The Everyday
Halogen Family
Cookbook

Also by Sarah Flower

The Everyday Halogen Oven Cookbook
Quick, easy and nutritious recipes for all the family

Halogen Cooking for Two

Perfect Baking with your Halogen Oven
How to create tasty bread, cupcakes, bakes, biscuits and savouries

Slow Cook, Fast Food
200 Healthy, wholesome slow cooker and one pot meals for all the family

Eat Well, Spend Less
200 quick, economical and healthy recipes for busy home cooks

Live More, Spend Less
A savvy guide to saving money for all the family

The Everyday Halogen Family Cookbook

Another 200 delicious meals and treats
from the author of
The Everyday Halogen Oven Cookbook

SARAH FLOWER

SPRING HILL

Published by Spring Hill, an imprint of How To Books Ltd.
Spring Hill House, Spring Hill Road
Begbroke, Oxford OX5 1RX
United Kingdom
Tel: (01865) 375794
Fax: (01865) 379162
info@howtobooks.co.uk
www.howtobooks.co.uk

First published 2011
Reprinted 2012

How To Books greatly reduce the carbon footprint of their books
by sourcing their typesetting and printing in the UK.

British Library Cataloguing in Publication Data
A catalogue record of this book is available from the British Library.

ISBN: 978 1 905862 70 2

Produced for How To Books by Deer Park Productions, Tavistock, Devon
Designed and typeset by Mousemat Design Ltd
Printed and bound in Great Britain by Bell & Bain Ltd, Glasgow

NOTE: The material contained in this book is set out in good faith for general
guidance and no liability can be accepted for loss or expense incurred as a result of
relying in particular circumstances on statements made in the book. Laws and
regulations are complex and liable to change, and readers should check the current
position with relevant authorities before making personal arrangements.

Contents

Introduction

I am thrilled that my first halogen cookbook, *The Everyday Halogen Oven Cookbook,* has been such a success and I sincerely hope this sequel will continue to inspire you. It has been incredibly rewarding to read some of the positive reviews and comments posted on the internet. I have also received so many lovely emails from readers, some with food queries, others just to let me know how they are getting on with the book. I am especially proud to be getting more emails from readers overseas – the US, Australia and New Zealand in particular.

I would like to start a forum for readers to share their experiences and recipes, so watch this space and keep an eye on my website: www.sarahflower.co.uk

As you may already know, I am a big fan of the halogen oven and I genuinely use it every day. My son, who is currently at university, also has a halogen – it is perfect for students! This little machine boasts a huge variety of skills – baking, roasting, steaming, defrosting, grilling and it can even wash itself! For those watching their weight, the halogen also drains the fat from meat, leaving you lean, mean joints that taste delicious and cook up to 40% faster than in a conventional oven.

Although, for me, the benefits of the halogen are not to do with speed. It is convenient, easy to use, and totally energy efficient and I love the fact that you have a perfect view of your creations while they cook. It has become part of my life and I would be lost without it.

I hope you enjoy this journey and if this book has whetted your appetite for halogen cookery, why not have a look at my other books in this series: *The Everyday Halogen Oven Cookbook, Perfect Baking with your Halogen Oven* and *Halogen Cooking For Two.*

Sarah x

Using Your Halogen Oven

As in my other halogen cookbooks, this first chapter shows newbie halogen oven users how to get the most from their machine. If you have bought another one of my books, you may want to skip this chapter as it contains duplicate information, or you might like to quickly scan it just to remind yourself of the joys of the halogen.

Choosing the right machine for you
There are many different halogen ovens on the market, but they are basically all the same machine. The two main variations are the bowl size and whether the lid is on a hinge. My first machine was from JML when they first started to become popular. I was not really sure what to expect and, over time, it has gained more and more use in our home. Personally I would opt for the largest bowl as this increases the oven's usability. You can also purchase extenders, which can help maximise use. Extenders are metal rings that fit over the top of the halogen bowl, literally extending the height of the bowl and enabling you to fit more into your oven. The lid then fits on top of the extender. They are also useful if you want to keep the food away from the heating elements to prevent burning.

After using the JML, I progressed to the Flavorwave Turbo Platinum Oven. Some of the advantages of this particular oven are that it has a hinged lid, digital settings, three-speed fan and a preheat setting.

Looking at online forums I have noticed that the lids do cause a bit of a bugbear. I used a lid stand positioned beside my JML machine, though annoyingly these are optional extras that you have to purchase and are quite flimsy to look at. Personally, I think it is better to buy the halogen cooker with the hinged lid if you can afford it – this is definitely a safer and easier option.

How do they work?

The halogen oven is basically a large glass bowl with an electric halogen lid. The lid is heavy as it contains the halogen element, timer and temperature settings. It can be fiddly to clean but I will come to that later. The halogen bulbs heat up the bowl and the fan moves the air around the bowl to create an even temperature. As it is smaller than a conventional oven, it heats up faster, reducing the need for long preheating and in some cases reducing the overall cooking time.

This makes it a very popular choice for those watching their pennies, living on their own or, like me, cooking for a busy family. It has even become a popular choice for students and caravanners. I read on a forum that some caravanners use the self-clean facility just like a mini dishwasher – ingenious! It is also popular as a second oven and really becomes invaluable at busy times like Christmas.

For safety, the lid's handle has to be in place (placed securely down) for the machine to turn on. This means that when you lift the lid, the oven is automatically turned off. If you are using the Flavorwave machine with the hinged lid, you have to press the start button and remember to turn the machine off when you lift the lid.

The halogen does cook slightly differently to a conventional oven, so first beginning to use it often involves a process of trial and error, but it is not vastly different. If you have favourite recipes that you cook in the conventional oven, try them in the halogen. I find cooking at a slightly lower temperature or cooking for less time normally gives the same results, but hopefully this book will help give you more confidence.

The halogen oven is not a microwave and does not work in the same way as a microwave, so if you are thinking you can cook food in minutes you are wrong. It does, however, have a multitude of functions – defrosting, baking, grilling, roasting and steaming are all perfect for the halogen. Remember that to get the optimum benefit, air needs to circulate around the bowl, so ideally place dishes and trays on racks and avoid the temptation to over fill.

Getting the right equipment

This sounds obvious but … make sure you have oven trays, baking sheets and casserole dishes that will fit inside your halogen oven. There is nothing more frustrating than planning a meal and just at the last minute realising that your dish does not fit in the machine! You can use any ovenproof dish or tray – metal, silicon and Pyrex are all fine. The halogen oven is round so it makes sense to look at trays and stands of the same shape, just smaller so you can remove them without burning yourself!

This is probably the only disadvantage of the halogen. When I first started using one, it was frustrating to find that 80% of my bakeware did not fit in the machine but a quick revamp and purchase of the accessories have proved invaluable. If money is tight, you will often find great casserole dishes at boot sales or charity shops – you don't have to spend a fortune on new cookware.

You can also buy an accessories pack, which contains steamer pans, grilling pans, toasting racks and even an extension ring. These are highly recommended if you use your oven regularly and certainly enhance what you can do with the machine. There are many websites selling or advertising these accessories, so a general internet search will point you in the right direction. Amazon is also a great place to look.

Let there be light

As experienced halogen users will know, the halogen light turns on and off during cooking. This is not a fault of the thermostat as some people have mentioned on forums. It literally turns off when the programmed temperature is reached, then on again when it drops. Set the temperature and marvel at how quickly the oven reaches the required temperature – literally in minutes. I love the light – along with being able to watch your food cook, there is something quite cosy about walking into your kitchen on a winter or autumn evening and seeing the glow of the halogen cooker.

Timings

The halogen oven comes with a 60-minute timer and temperature setting dials. The Flavorwave Turbo also comes with three fan settings and a digital timer. All halogens turn off when the timer settings have been reached. This means that you can be reassured that if the phone rings or you are called away from the kitchen, your food won't spoil.

Size

The oven is small enough to sit on a worktop, but do allow space for removal of the lid if it is not hinged. The lid can get very hot and is quite large and heavy, being the brains of the machine, so it can be a good idea to buy the lid stand. However, be careful when using this stand as it can seem quite flimsy until you get used to it. You could opt to place the lid on a heatproof surface but, again, be careful not to burn yourself or your worktop!

Careful does it

Your oven should come with some tong type of gadget to help you lift out the racks. They are quite useful, but I also use a more substantial set of tongs. As with any oven or cooker, do be careful as the bowl and contents get very hot. I find using proper oven gloves a necessity as they cover your whole hand and wrist and can prevent accidents.

As with all electrical and hot appliances, do not let your children near the halogen – the glass bowl gets very hot.

Foil and coverings

Some people like to use foil when cooking. This can be a good idea as it prevents food from browning too quickly or it can be used to parcel foods, but make sure the foil is secure. The fan is very strong and if the foil is not secure it could float around the oven and might damage the element. Another option for preventing burning is obviously to turn the temperature down or place the food further away from the element (use the low rack or add an extension ring).

Cleaning your oven

Your oven is promoted as being self-cleaning. This basically means that you fill it with a little water and a squirt of washing-up liquid and then turn it on to the wash setting. The combination of the fan and the heat allows the water to swish around the bowl giving it a quick clean. This normally takes about 10 minutes. Personally I find it just as simple to remove the bowl and place it in the dishwasher – it always comes out gleaming.

The lid is a little more difficult to clean and I would refer to the manufacturer's guidelines as each product differs a little. Do not get the element or electrical parts wet!

High and low racks

There are two standard racks which come with every halogen oven – a high and a low rack. The high rack is placed nearer the element so use this if you want to brown something. The low rack is used more for longer cooking times.

You can cook directly on the bottom of the bowl. I do this quite often, particularly if I am being lazy and just want to chuck in some oven chips or if I am roasting something. It does cook well but takes a little longer than using the racks, as air is not able to circulate all around the food.

Grilling

If you want to grill something you really need to place the rack as high as possible. The two racks (low and high) that come with the halogen oven may not be suitable for quick grilling – though if this is all you have it will work, but just take longer. I purchased an accessory pack and in this you get a toasting rack (with egg holes), which can be used as a grilling rack, either on its own or with a baking tray on top.

As you are cooking close to the element, grilling times are much quicker, for example you can grill cheese on toast in approximately 3–4 minutes.

Baking

Some people worry about using the halogen to bake cakes but I think this is because they are setting the oven temperature too high, resulting in a crusty brown cake top with a soggy middle. Setting the oven to a lower temperature can solve this problem. Muffins and cupcakes take between 12 and 18 minutes. You only really encounter problems with cakes if you are cooking for too long at too high a temperature. Try some of my cake recipes and you will see how simple it can be.

Preheat or not to preheat

Most recipes I have found on forums don't mention preheating the oven. This is probably due to how quickly the oven reaches its temperature setting. However, I think it is worth turning the oven on a few minutes before use just to bring it up to the right temperature.

I found this to be the case when attempting to cook soft-boiled eggs. According to the Flavorwave recipe book, I should be able to cook a soft egg in 6 minutes just by placing it on the high rack. It didn't work, but when I tried again in a heated oven it was much more successful. As the halogen only takes a few minutes to reach the set temperature, I believe it is best to preheat and therefore most of my recipes advise this.

Some machines (such as the Flavorwave) have a preheat button which preheats at 260°C for 6 minutes, but others, such as the JML, require you to set the oven to the required temperature and then turn it on.

I hope this chapter has not confused you. Move on to try some recipes and then come back to this chapter at a later date – it will probably make more sense then!

Enjoy!

WEIGHT	
Metric (approx.)	Imperial
25–30g	1oz
50–55g	2oz
85g	3oz
100g	3.5oz
125g	4oz
150g	5oz
175g	6oz
200g	7oz
225g	8oz
250g	9oz
280g	10oz
350g	12oz
400g	14oz
450g	16oz/1lb
900kg	2lb

LIQUID MEASURE	
Metric (approx.)	Imperial
5ml	1 teaspoon (tsp)
15ml	1 tablespoon (tbsp)
25–30ml	1 fl oz
50ml	2 fl oz
75ml	3 fl oz
100–125ml	4 fl oz
150ml	5 fl oz
175ml	6 fl oz
200ml	7 fl oz
225ml	8 fl oz
250ml	9 fl oz
300ml	10 fl oz (½ pint)
600ml	20 fl oz (1 pint)
1 litre	1¾ pints

Snacks, Side Dishes and Accompaniments

Halogen ovens aren't just for main meals or desserts, they are perfect for quick and easy snacks. I included quite a comprehensive list of snacks in my *Everyday Halogen Oven Cookbook*, including the basics such as toast, bacon, garlic bread and frozen chips, but here are some other varieties and suggestions, along with some simple tips you can adapt to suit.

Unlike microwaves, halogen ovens can heat up pastries, pizzas and snacks without resulting in a soggy mess. They can also make delicious toasties, warmed bagels, bruschetta, and even boil an egg! Don't forget you can steam, bake, roast or grill vegetables, and here are some great suggestions to help enhance your cooking experience.

SERVES 1–2

1–2 tablespoons milk
10g butter
60g mature cheese
½ small onion, finely
    chopped (or a few
    spring onions)
1 teaspoon mustard
Black pepper
1–2 slices bread
1–2 slices bacon
2–3 slices tomato
Seasoning

Bacon and Tomato Welsh Rarebit

A new take on the Welsh rarebit – perfect for using up any leftovers!

• In a saucepan, put the milk, butter, cheese, onion and mustard and stir until dissolved and thick. Season with black pepper. Be careful not to have this too high or it will stick and burn.

• Spoon the cheese mixture onto one side of the bread and season to taste. Place on the grill rack (see the Grilling section in Chapter 1 for tips) and set the halogen to 250°C.

• Place the slice of bacon next to the bread (not on top) and cook both for 3–4 minutes until the cheese mixture is golden and bubbling and the bacon is starting to crisp – you may want to continue cooking the bacon for longer if you like it really crisp.

• Remove from the oven. Place a slice or two of tomato on the rarebit, followed by the bacon. Season to taste.

• Serve with a side salad and some delicious chutney.

Blue Cheese and Spinach Rarebit

SERVES 2

- Lightly toast your bread – you only want a light golden, not quite toasted effect, as it will continue to brown when placed in the halogen.
- While the bread is toasting, place the spinach in a colander and run under hot water until it wilts. Squeeze to remove any excess moisture.
- Place the spinach leaves in a bowl and add all remaining ingredients. Combine well.
- Divide the mixture between each slice of toast and press down firmly.
- Place the toast on the grill rack (see the Grilling section in Chapter 1 for tips) and set the halogen to 250°C. Toast for 3–5 minutes until it starts to brown and bubble. Serve immediately.

2–4 slices wholegrain bread
100g baby leaf spinach
100ml crème fraîche
75g blue cheese, crumbled
1 teaspoon wholegrain mustard
Black pepper

SUITABLE FOR VEGETARIANS

SERVES 1–2

2 slices wholemeal
bread
Butter
2–3 slices turkey breast
1–2 teaspoons
cranberry sauce
Seasoning

Turkey and Cranberry Toastie

This is not just a recipe for Christmas!

- Place the bread on the grill rack (see the Grilling section in Chapter 1 for tips) and cook at 250°C for 3–4 minutes until it starts to golden.
- Remove and butter the toast. Cover one slice with the turkey and cranberry sauce. Sandwich together.
- Place back on the grill rack and cook again for 2–3 minutes.
- Serve immediately with a lovely rocket salad garnish.

Bacon, Rocket and Tomato Deluxe

SERVES 2–3

- Brush the bacon with a little olive oil and place on a browning tray on the grill rack (see the Grilling section in Chapter 1 for tips). Set the halogen to 250°C.
- Cook until the bacon reaches your desired crispiness (5–8 minutes, turning over halfway through).
- When almost cooked, place the French bread or bagel alongside the bacon for a minute or two, as this will start to warm/toast one side of the bread.
- Remove when ready and plate up: place the bacon on top of the bread, cover with the tomato slices and finish with the rocket. Season and if you are a fan of olive oil, drizzle with some extra virgin olive oil. Serve immediately.

Olive oil
2–4 rashers bacon (depending on appetite!)
1–2 slices/portions French bread or bagel
1–2 tomatoes, thickly sliced
Handful of rocket (or lettuce if you prefer)
Seasoning to taste

SERVES 2-4

250g whole
   Camembert cheese

SUITABLE FOR VEGETARIANS

Baked Camembert

I'm a bit embarrassed to call this a recipe, but once you've tasted it you will understand why it is a favourite.

- If your Camembert comes in a wooden box, remove all packaging before placing the camembert back into the box. Alternatively you can wrap in foil and place on a baking tray. I actually have a little ovenware pot that came with some Camembert which I reuse.
- Place on the high rack and bake at 210°C for 10–12 minutes.
- Serve with a selection of vegetable sticks, crusty bread or lightly steamed asparagus spears.

Muffin Pizzas

SERVES 2–4

These are so easy to prepare, it makes you wonder why we bother messing around with pizza dough. Kids love them if you get them to decorate the tops to resemble faces. Feel free to use whatever topping you desire. This is a basic recipe using just cheese and tomato – the rest is up to you!

- Place the muffins ready to assemble on a worktop or tray. Add a layer of the pasta sauce (my cheat's way!) followed by any other ingredients you require and finish with a generous handful of grated cheese. Season to taste.
- Place the muffins directly on the grill rack or on a browning tray if you prefer (see the Grilling section in Chapter 1 for tips). Set the temperature to 250°C and cook for 5–7 minutes until golden and bubbling. Serve immediately.

1–2 muffins, cut in
   half
2–4 spoonfuls pasta
   sauce
Mature Cheddar,
   grated
Black pepper to
   season

SUITABLE FOR VEGETARIANS

SERVES 1–2

2 slices wholemeal
   bread
1–2 teaspoons
   wholegrain mustard
2–4 slices Parma ham
2–4 slices tomato
Handful of rocket
Seasoning
Olive oil

Parma Ham and Mustard Bruschetta

Simple but delicious!

- Place the slices of bread on the grill rack (see the Grilling section in Chapter 1 for tips) and set the halogen to 250°C. Cook for 4–5 minutes to toast until golden.
- Remove from the oven and spread with wholegrain mustard. Top with the ham, slice of tomato and handful of rocket.
- Season to taste and drizzle with olive oil before serving.

Tuna Melt Panini

Create your own café-favourite snack in your halogen.

1 small tin tuna
Mayonnaise
Cheddar, grated
Seasoning
1–2 panini rolls

- In a bowl, mix the tuna, mayonnaise (enough to reach a creamy consistency) and Cheddar to taste. Season well.
- Slice open your panini rolls and fill with tuna mixture. Place the tops back on.
- Place them on the grill rack (see the Grilling section in Chapter 1 for tips) and set the halogen to 250°C. Cook for 4–6 minutes until golden and the tuna/cheese has started to melt.
- Serve with a side salad and tortilla chips.

Stuffed Pitta

SERVES 1–2

1–2 pitta
Cheese, grated
Carrot, grated
Onion, sliced
Peppers, sliced
2–3 tablespoons
  hummus
Seasoning

SUITABLE FOR VEGETARIANS

This is really simple. Here is the recipe my sons love best, but feel free to fill with your own variations.

• Brush the pitta with a little water before placing on the grill rack of the halogen (see the Grilling section in Chapter 1 for tips). Turn the halogen on to 250°C.
• Cook for 4–5 minutes until it puffs up a little and goes a little darker. Don't overcook as it can become too crispy and dry.
• Using a sharp knife, slit the pitta open and stuff with the remaining ingredients.
• Season to taste and serve immediately.

Mozzarella, Sundried Tomato and Rocket Bagel

This is my favourite bagel combination. Perfect with a lovely sesame or seeded bagel.

- Place the bagels on the grill rack (see the Grilling section in Chapter 1 for tips) and set the halogen to 250°C. Cook for 4–5 minutes until they start to brown.
- Remove from the oven and add the mozzarella, sundried tomatoes and rocket.
- Season to taste. Serve immediately whilst still warm!

SERVES 1–2

1–2 bagels
2–3 slices mozzarella
3–6 sundried tomatoes
(drained of oil)
Rocket
Seasoning

SUITABLE FOR VEGETARIANS

SERVES 2

3–4 cloves garlic, finely chopped
100g button mushrooms
1 dessertspoon butter
200g crème fraîche
Small handful of parsley, chopped
Seasoning
4–6 slices ciabatta bread, thickly sliced

SUITABLE FOR VEGETARIANS

Creamy Mushrooms

You can make this in advance and serve with mashed potato or on thick, crusty toast as a delicious snack, starter or even a main meal.

- In a sauté pan, put the garlic, mushrooms and butter and cook until the mushrooms start to soften. Add the crème fraîche and stir well. Add the chopped parsley and season to taste.
- When the sauce is done, keep it warm on a low heat and, meanwhile, slice the ciabatta and place on the grill rack of the halogen oven (see the Grilling section in Chapter 1 for tips).
- Set the temperature to 250°C and grill until it starts to brown. Serve immediately.

Roasted Red Pepper Hummus

SERVES 4–6

- Place the halved peppers on a greased baking tray. Drizzle with a little olive oil and season to taste.
- Place on the high rack and cook at 200°C for 30 minutes.
- Remove the peppers from the oven and place in a food processor. Add all the remaining ingredients except for the optional lemon juice and whizz.
- Add more oil or lemon juice until you have the desired consistency. Don't worry if it does not taste too garlicky. You really should allow it to rest for at least 15 minutes before you will taste the richness of the garlic – add more at that stage if you feel it's necessary.
- Serve chilled.

2 red peppers, halved
Seasoning
2 x 400g tin chickpeas
3–4 cloves garlic
2 tablespoons tahini
  (sesame seed paste)
3–4 tablespoons olive
  oil
Lemon juice
  (optional)

SUITABLE FOR VEGETARIANS

SERVES 4–6

8 tomatoes, halved
4–5 cloves garlic, finely
  sliced
Small handful of
  thyme
Olive oil
Balsamic vinegar
Sea salt
Black pepper

SUITABLE FOR VEGETARIANS

Roasted Tomatoes

I had these when I visited Djerba, Tunisia and they were absolutely delicious, especially for breakfast with some freshly scrambled eggs and rye bread.

- Place the halved tomatoes on a baking tray. Sprinkle with the sliced garlic and randomly distribute the thyme.
- Drizzle with olive oil and a dash of balsamic vinegar. Finish with sea salt and black pepper.
- Place on the high rack and cook at 180°C for 10 minutes.
- Serve hot or cold, or leave a little longer in the oven until really soft and purée up to make a rich tomato sauce ideal for pasta or even soups.

Crab, Garlic and Chilli Mini Toasties

SERVES 4–6

- Place the sliced bread flat-side down on a baking tray. Drizzle with garlic oil.
- Place on the grill rack (see the Grilling section in Chapter 1 for tips) and cook at 240°C for 5–7 minutes until the bread starts to golden.
- Meanwhile, mix the remaining ingredients except for the paprika together.
- When the bread is cooked, place the crab mixture onto the mini toasts. Finish with a sprinkle of paprika and serve immediately.

1 small baguette, sliced
Drizzle of garlic olive oil
2 cloves garlic, crushed
1 chilli, finely chopped
Zest of ½ lemon
125g crabmeat
Seasoning
Paprika

Cheese, Onion and Bacon Mini Frittatas

SERVES 4–6

Olive oil
4–5 spring onions,
   finely chopped
½ pack lean bacon,
   chopped
6 eggs
40ml double cream
   (optional)
125g mature cheese
   (Cheddar works
   well)
Black pepper
Sea salt
1 teaspoon dried
   oregano

Great hot or cold.

- Heat the oil in a sauté pan. Add the onion and bacon and cook for 5 minutes.
- Whilst that is cooking, beat the eggs in a jug. Add the cream and cheese.
- Season with black pepper and sea salt, and add the oregano.
- Stir in the onion and bacon.
- Grease your silicon muffin cases and place them onto a baking tray. It helps to keep them stable if you place them tightly together.
- Pour the mixture into the muffin cases.
- Place the tray on the high rack. Set the temperature to 200°C and cook for 15–20 minutes, until golden and almost set. Serve hot or cold.

Hot Courgette, Garlic and Parmesan Salad

SERVES 2

- Place the sliced courgettes in a shallow ovenproof dish. Sprinkle with garlic, drizzle with olive oil and season with black pepper.
- Place the dish on the grill rack (see the Grilling section in Chapter 1 for tips).
- Set the temperature to 250°C and cook for 7–10 minutes, until browned.
- Remove and add Parmesan shavings. Serve immediately.

3 courgettes, sliced
2–3 cloves garlic,
  finely sliced
Olive oil
Black pepper
Parmesan shavings

SUITABLE FOR VEGETARIANS

Bacon, Onion and Cheese Scones

SERVES 6–8

Olive oil
½ pack lean bacon, diced
1 small onion, finely chopped
250g self-raising flour
50g butter
75g mature Cheddar
25g red Leicester
1 egg, beaten
100ml buttermilk
Black pepper

- Heat the oil in a sauté pan. Add the bacon and onion and cook until the onion is soft. Remove from the heat and leave to one side.
- Place the flour in a bowl. Rub in the butter thoroughly.
- Add the cheese, bacon and onion and combine well.
- In a jug mix the egg with the buttermilk. Add this to the flour mixture and combine until it forms a dough. This might be a bit sticky so you will need a floured surface.
- Place the dough on the floured surface and roughly pat into a slab about 3cm thick.
- Using cutters, cut rounds and place these on your greased or lined baking tray.
- Brush with a little milk or a beaten egg – if you like a golden top you could grate a little more red Leicester on the top of each scone.
- Place on the high rack and cook at 210°C for 12–18 minutes until golden.
- Serve hot or cold. Delicious with some cheese and homemade chutney.

Foil-baked Herby Vegetables

SERVES 2–4

- Cut a double layer square of foil, big enough to house your vegetables.
- Brush the foil with garlic-infused olive oil. Bring the sides of the foil up to form a bucket shape to contain the vegetables.
- Add the vegetables and herbs. Season to taste with black pepper and sea salt. Add the butter and water and a drizzle of garlic-infused olive oil. Seal well.
- Place the parcel on the low rack and cook at 160°C for 40–50 minutes or until the vegetables are cooked. Serve immediately.

Garlic-infused olive oil
2 carrots, cut into
   batons
2 sweet potatoes, cut
   into batons
2 courgettes, sliced
1 red pepper, sliced
1 onion, sliced
6 new potatoes,
   quartered
5 cherry tomatoes
Handful of assorted
   fresh herbs (basil,
   rosemary, chives,
   oregano, thyme)
Black pepper
Sea salt
1 knob of butter
4 tablespoons water

SUITABLE FOR VEGETARIANS

MAKES 30 MINI BISCUITS

150g plain flour
150g butter
100g mature Cheddar,
    grated
50g red Leicester
    cheese, grated
Pinch of cayenne
    pepper
Black pepper
1 egg yolk

SUITABLE FOR VEGETARIANS

Cheese Biscuits

- In a bowl, rub the butter into the flour. Add the grated cheese, cayenne pepper and season with black pepper.
- Add the egg yolk and combine well. Leave to rest in the fridge for 30 minutes.
- When you are ready to cook, roll the dough out onto a floured board to a thickness of approximately 5mm. Then cut with small biscuit cutters. I normally use 4cm round biscuit cutters or little star shapes. You can make them bigger if you prefer.
- Place the cut biscuits onto a greased baking tray. Because of the quantity of biscuits this recipe makes, you will have to cook them in batches.
- Place on the high rack. Set the temperature to 210°C and cook for 8–12 minutes until golden. Chill on a cooling rack.
- Serve with sweet chilli sauce. Delicious!

Note: You can use this recipe to make Cheese Straws.

Spicy Potato Wedges

SERVES 4

- Place the potatoes in a bowl. Add the chilli, garlic, paprika and thyme.
- Season with black pepper and sea salt. Drizzle with oil and toss until well combined.
- Pour this onto your browning tray. Place on the high rack and cook at 210°C for 20–25 minutes, turning and adding more oil if necessary halfway through cooking.
- Remove from the oven and place in a serving dish. Sprinkle with chilli flakes, sea salt and a little more thyme. Serve immediately.

3 baking potatoes, cut into wedges
3 sweet potatoes, cut into wedges
1 chilli, finely chopped
2–3 cloves garlic, crushed
1 teaspoon paprika
1 teaspoon dried thyme
Black pepper
Sea salt
Chilli-infused olive oil
Dried chilli flakes

SUITABLE FOR VEGETARIANS

Soups

These recipes are intended to demonstrate how versatile the halogen really is. Yes, soups are best cooked in a slow cooker or saucepan, but why not try something different. The flavours of roasted vegetables, for which the halogen is perfect, are amazing and really add a special touch to soups.

1 white onion, finely
chopped
25g butter
1 stick celery, finely
diced
1 medium potato,
finely diced
800ml–1 litre hot
water or hot
vegetable stock (low
salt as the cheese is
very salty)
150g blue cheese
Seasoning

SUITABLE FOR VEGETARIANS

Celery and Blue Cheese Soup

This is a lovely soup with a fantastic flavour. You can cook it on the hob if you prefer, but it works equally well in your halogen as described below. Feel free to season to your taste.

- Into a casserole dish (first make sure it fits in the halogen), put the onion, butter, celery and potato. Place on the high rack (or low rack if your dish is too big to fit) and turn the temperature to 220°C. Cook for 5–8 minutes, stirring occasionally to distribute and help soften.
- Add the water or stock. Cover with a lid or double thickness of tin foil (making sure this is secure) and continue to cook for 30 minutes.
- Remove the lid and check to see if the diced vegetables are soft. Once soft, add the blue cheese and season to taste. If you like a creamier soup, you can add a dollop or two of crème fraîche or thick Greek yoghurt, though personally I don't think the soup needs it.
- Use an electric stick blender and whizz until smooth. Season to taste.
- Serve immediately or remove and leave to one side until needed. It freezes well or keeps in an airtight container in the fridge for 2–3 days.

Slow-baked Tomato, Pepper and Basil Soup

SERVES 4

This is a really tasty soup. If you want a more wholesome soup, you could add 50–75g of dried red lentils. Boil them in water until soft and then add the lentils with the water (as indicated below) and whizz until smooth.

- Place the chopped tomatoes, pepper and garlic in an ovenproof dish. Sprinkle with sea salt, sugar and basil leaves (or thyme if you prefer) and drizzle with a light splatter of olive oil.
- Turn the halogen oven to 160°C, place on the high rack and cook for 30 minutes.
- Remove the vegetables from the halogen cooker and mix in your stock or water. Add more water or stock if necessary (or your cooked lentils and stock/water). Add the tomato paste and chopped basil. Whizz until smooth with an electric hand blender. Season to taste.
- Serve with fresh bread for a tasty lunch or light evening meal.

8 tomatoes, quartered
1 red pepper, quartered
2–4 cloves garlic, crushed
Sprinkle of sea salt
Sprinkle of sugar
Small handful of fresh basil leaves (or thyme)
Drizzle of olive oil
500ml vegetable stock or water
1 teaspoon sundried tomato paste
2–3 teaspoons fresh basil, chopped
Seasoning to taste

SUITABLE FOR VEGETARIANS AND VEGANS

SERVES 4

110g pack chorizo
   sausage
1 red onion, finely
   chopped
2 cloves garlic,
   crushed
½ teaspoon chilli flakes
1 tin chopped
   tomatoes
300ml vegetable stock
1 tin haricot beans
¼ savoy cabbage,
   shredded

Chorizo, Cabbage and Bean Soup

A really wholesome, filling soup, perfect for cold winter days.

- Dice the chorizo after removing the skin, as this can be unpleasant if left.
- Place the onion, garlic, chilli flakes and chorizo in an ovenproof dish, first making sure this fits well in your halogen oven. Later in the recipe you will need to use a lid, so make sure you have this to hand. (If your dish does not have a lid, use a double layer of foil held securely.)
- Turn the temperature to 220°C, place the dish on the low rack and cook for 10 minutes, stirring occasionally to ensure the onion starts to soften and does not burn. The oil will ooze from the sausage so you should not need to add more oil.
- Once soft, add all the remaining ingredients and season to taste. Cover with your lid (or secure tin foil) and cook for another 20–25 minutes.
- Serve with crusty bread. Delicious!

Roasted Pumpkin Soup

This makes a delicious treat for Halloween or, for an all-year-round treat, you can use other squash.

- Preheat the oven using the preheat setting or set the temperature to 210°C.
- Cut the pumpkin and sweet potato into wedges. Place on a baking tray with the carrot. Lightly brush with oil. Add the garlic, onion and spices. Combine well.
- Place on the low rack and bake for 20–25 minutes.
- Remove the flesh from the pumpkin wedges and roughly chop the roasted vegetables. Add with the onion/seasoning mix to a casserole dish. Add all the remaining ingredients and combine well.
- Place the casserole dish on the low rack. Cover with a lid or with tinfoil secured tightly. Cook at 200°C for 30–40 minutes.
- Allow to cool slightly and then use an electric hand blender to purée. Season as required.
- For impressive presentation, use hollowed out pumpkins as serving dishes.

SERVES 4–6

1 small pumpkin
1 medium sweet potato
1–2 carrots, thickly chopped
Olive oil
1–2 cloves garlic, crushed
1 onion, cut into wedges
1 teaspoon root ginger, grated
1 teaspoon nutmeg, grated
1 teaspoon ground coriander
2 sticks celery
4 tomatoes, peeled and chopped
2 teaspoons tomato purée (optional)
300–425ml water or stock
15ml lemon juice
Seasoning

SUITABLE FOR VEGETARIANS AND VEGANS

Tomato, Chilli and Ginger soup

SERVES 4

3–4 tomatoes, quartered

1 red pepper, roughly quartered

3–4 cloves garlic, left whole

2.5cm knuckle of ginger

1 red chilli, quartered

1–2 tablespoons olive oil

1 tablespoon balsamic vinegar

Sprinkle of sea salt

Sprinkle of sugar

Generous grind of black pepper

1 carrot

1 stick celery

Knob of butter

350ml boiling water

50g red lentils

SUITABLE FOR VEGETARIANS

I developed this recipe when I was feeling under par. I really fancied a nourishing soup with a bit of a kick. The key was to make a healthy soup without too much effort and to make it quickly. If you don't want the additional heat, you can omit the ginger, but do keep the chilli as it does give a really nice flavour.

• Place the tomato, pepper, garlic, ginger and chilli in an ovenproof dish. Drizzle with olive oil, balsamic vinegar, sprinkle with sea salt and sugar, and finish with a grind of black pepper. Combine gently.

• Place on the high rack and set the temperature to 190°C and cook for 15–20 minutes.

• Meanwhile boil the kettle, turn the heat on the stove and dice the carrot and celery into small pieces. Place the carrot and celery in a pan with a knob of butter and sweat for 5 minutes.

• Add the boiling water and lentils and cook for 10 more minutes.

• When the halogen timer beeps, remove the tomato mixture and add this to the saucepan. Cook for another 5 minutes before liquidising with a hand/stick blender. If you want a thinner soup, add more liquid.

• Serve immediately or this soup can be kept in the fridge or frozen.

Roasted Garlic and Red Pepper Soup

SERVES 4

- Place the halved red peppers on a baking tray. You can squash them in to make them fit.
- Place the halved bulb of garlic in the centre of the baking tray – do not peel the garlic. Drizzle with olive oil and season to taste.
- Place on the high rack of the halogen and set the temperature to 190°C. Cook for 20 minutes until the peppers start to soften.
- Remove and add the tomatoes. Continue to cook for another 10 minutes.
- Remove from the halogen and place the peppers and tomatoes in a saucepan. Add the flesh of the garlic, discarding the skin.
- Add the stock or water, and tomato paste. Add the chopped basil. Season to taste and cook on a low heat for 10 minutes.
- For a smooth soup use an electric blender and whizz until blended.
- Serve with warm crusty bread and hummus.

4 large red peppers, halved and deseeded
½ bulb garlic, left unpeeled
Olive oil
Black pepper
Sea salt
6 tomatoes
300ml vegetable stock or water
2 teaspoons sundried tomato paste
Handful of fresh basil leaves, chopped

SUITABLE FOR VEGETARIANS AND VEGANS

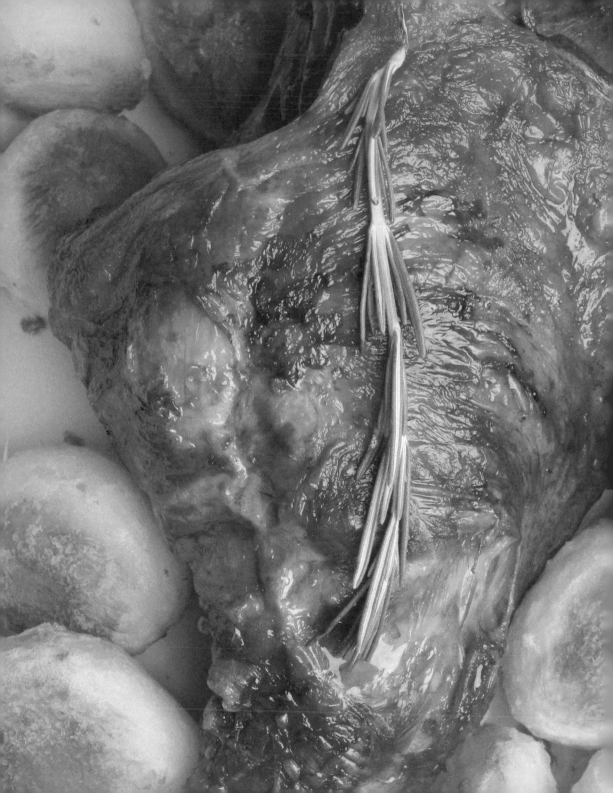

Meat

The halogen oven can cook meat slightly quicker than the conventional oven, though you have to be careful to get your temperature settings right. Too high and the top of the joint or bird will burn whilst the middle may remain raw or undercooked. I would advise using a temperature gauge to test your meat during cooking, particularly poultry or joints of meat, until you are more confident – even when following a recipe.

When meat is cooked on the lower rack, the juices and fats drain away therefore making the meat healthier. Some people worry that the meat will dry out too much, but to be honest, meat does tend to be very tender and moist when cooked in the halogen – unless you overcook it! If you are concerned, you can always place your meat on a baking tray or even cook on the base of the halogen, which is ideal if you want to add roast potatoes.

You can cook a joint as you would do in a conventional oven: roughly 20 minutes per 500g at 180°C and add another 10 minutes to the end of the cooking time.

As with all foods cooked in the halogen, make sure there is adequate space between the element and the food – ideally at least 2–3cm. The nearer food is to the element the more likely it is to burn or cook quickly. If you are concerned, wrap some foil over the food for the first half of the cooking time, though make sure it is secured well as the power of the fan could lift it.

100g fresh
  breadcrumbs
550ml milk
1 onion, halved or
  quartered
1 bay leaf
1 teaspoon wholegrain
  mustard
4 eggs
150g lean bacon,
  chopped
125g mature Cheddar,
  grated
1 teaspoon dried
  thyme or small
  handful fresh thyme,
  chopped
Seasoning to taste

Cheese, Bacon and Onion Puff

This is a light dish with a consistency similar to a soufflé.
Makes a nice one-pot, supper-time dish using basic store
ingredients. Very retro!

- Place the breadcrumbs in a bowl.
- Place the milk, onion and bay leaf in a pan and bring
  to the boil.
- Remove the onion (leaving it to onc side) and bay
  leaf and stir in the mustard. Pour this over the
  breadcrumbs and leave to stand for 20–30 minutes.
- Separate the eggs. Mix the yolks and all other
  ingredients (leaving aside the egg whites) together
  with the soaked breadcrumbs. Chop the onion finely
  and add to the mixture.
- Beat the egg whites until light and fluffy. Fold into
  the mixture carefully.
- Pour this into a well greased ovenproof dish. Turn on
  the halogen to 200°C and bake on the low rack for
  25–35 minutes.
- Serve with a green salad.

Moussaka

- Place the aubergine in a pan of boiling water for 2 minutes. Then remove and pat dry. Leave to one side.
- Meanwhile, heat a little olive oil in a sauté pan and fry the onion and garlic. Add the lamb mince and cook until brown.
- Add the tomatoes, tomato purée, mint, cinnamon and seasoning and cook for another 2–3 minutes.
- Select your ovenproof dish – I normally use a Pyrex or lasagna dish for this. Make sure it fits into your halogen cooker.
- Place a layer of mince in your dish, followed by a layer of aubergine. Continue alternating mince and aubergine, finishing with a layer of mince.
- Mix the crème fraîche with the grated cheese and pour over the final layer of mince. Garnish with a sprinkle of Parmesan.
- Place on the low rack and set your halogen to 210°C. Cook for 20–25 minutes until bubbling.

2–3 aubergines, sliced
Olive oil
1 onion
2 cloves garlic, crushed
400g lamb mince
1 tin chopped tomatoes
2 teaspoons tomato purée
1 teaspoon dried mint
2 teaspoons cinnamon powder
Seasoning to taste
300ml low fat crème fraîche
50g mature Cheddar or Parmesan cheese, grated

Chicken, Goat's Cheese, Red Pepper and Cherry Tomato Bake

SERVES 4

4 chicken breasts
110g goat's cheese
Black pepper
1 punnet cherry
  tomatoes, halved
2 red peppers, thickly
  sliced
2 red onions, cut into
  wedges
Olive oil
Balsamic vinegar
Sea salt
Sugar

- Wash the chicken breasts. Using a very sharp knife, slit open one side of the breast to form a pocket. Fill with some of the goat's cheese. Repeat, stuffing the remaining chicken breasts.
- Place the chicken breasts in an ovenproof dish (making sure it fits in your halogen oven). Season to taste.
- Place the cherry tomatoes, peppers and red onion around the chicken. Drizzle the vegetables with olive oil and balsamic vinegar and finish with a sprinkle of sea salt and sugar.
- Place on the high rack and bake at 200°C for 20–25 minutes until golden.
- Serve with a lovely green salad.

Chilli and Lemongrass Chicken Kebabs

This is a great simple supper if you want to plan ahead and enjoy some free time away from the kitchen. Marinate the chicken whilst soaking the kebab sticks overnight or for a few hours before needed. Easy to prepare, just serve the kebabs with fluffy rice and salad.

1 stalk lemongrass
1–2 chillies
2–3 garlic cloves
Small handful of
   coriander leaves
1 tablespoon olive oil
Juice of 1 lime
4 chicken breasts, cut
   into large chunks

- If you have a food processor or mini processor, this can make your life so much easier. Simply put all the ingredients apart from the chicken into your processor and whizz to form a paste. If you don't have a processor, finely chop the ingredients (if you have a pestle and mortar this can help combine), add the oil and lime juice and combine well.
- Place the mixture in a bowl or freezer bag. Add the chicken chunks and marinate overnight or for 3–4 hours before cooking. At the same time, soak your kebab sticks as this prevents them from burning.
- When ready to prepare, simply place the chicken on the kebab sticks – you could alternate each chicken chunk with a cherry tomato or wedge of red pepper.
- Place the kebabs on the grill rack as you are effectively going to grill them. (See the Grilling section in Chapter 1 for tips.)
- Turn the heat up to the highest setting and grill, turning regularly to make sure the chicken is cooking well without burning. This should take no more than 10 minutes.
- Serve with fluffed-up rice and a lovely salad – perfect, yet so simple!

Cajun Chicken with Roasted Sweet Potatoes

6 sweet potatoes, cut
into thick wedges
(skins left on)
2 red onions, cut into
wedges
Olive oil
Paprika
Sea salt
Black pepper
4–6 chicken breasts
2–3 tablespoons Cajun
spice
1 tablespoon runny
honey
Juice and zest of 1
lime

- Place the sweet potato and onion wedges in an
ovenproof dish (first making sure it fits in your
halogen) and sprinkle with olive oil. Toss to ensure
they are evenly coated. Sprinkle with paprika, sea salt
and black pepper.
- Place on the high rack and cook at 200°C for 10
minutes.
- Meanwhile, score the chicken breasts with a sharp
knife. Combine the Cajun spice with the honey and
lime juice and zest. Using a pastry brush, coat the
chicken breasts thoroughly.
- Remove the tray from the halogen and add the
chicken breasts to the potato and onion wedges. If
you have more Cajun mixture left, you can also coat
the potatoes.
- Return to the high rack and cook for another 15–20
minutes, or until the chicken is cooked thoroughly.
- Serve with green salad.

Paprika Pork

SERVES 4

- Drizzle a little olive oil in an ovenproof dish and heat on your hob. Add the onion and green pepper and fry for 5–8 minutes, stirring regularly until they start to soften.
- Add the pork to the pan and brown all over.
- Stir in the paprika and cook for 1 minute. Then add the stock and allow to simmer gently for 10 minutes.
- Cover the dish with a lid or double layer of foil, securely tied. Then place on the high rack and cook at 180°C for 30–40 minutes until the pork is tender.
- Remove from oven and stir in the crème fraîche.
- Sprinkle with freshly chopped parsley and serve with rice or new potatoes and vegetables.

Olive oil
3 red onions, sliced
1 green pepper, sliced
500g pork, diced
3 teaspoons paprika
400ml chicken or
  vegetable stock
150g crème fraîche
Handful of parsley,
  chopped

SERVES 4

2 punnets cherry
  tomatoes
3 cloves garlic, left
  whole
1 pack thick bacon,
  roughly chopped
Olive oil
Sea salt
Black pepper
4 large eggs
2 tablespoons parsley,
  chopped

Pan-roasted Breakfast

Don't think this is only suitable for breakfast – it's ideal for a lovely supper, especially when you require comfort food.

• Place the tomatoes, garlic and bacon in your ovenproof dish (first making sure it fits in your halogen). Sprinkle with olive oil, sea salt and black pepper.
• Place on the high rack at 200°C for 10 minutes.
• Remove from the oven. Make 4 spaces evenly in the mixture and crack an egg into each space.
• Cover the dish with foil or a lid and bake for a further 10–15 minutes until the eggs are cooked to your taste.
• Remove from the oven and sprinkle over the parsley. Serve immediately with warm crusty bread.

Spicy Chicken

SERVES 4

This is a lovely, simple dish, made all the easier if you have a food processor. Simply whizz up the spices, leave to marinate with the chicken overnight or for at least 2–3 hours, then cook for 20–30 minutes. I serve it on a bed of pilau rice, mixed with peas and chopped onion. Delicious.

- Into your food processor, put all the ingredients apart from the chicken. Whizz to form a paste. Place the mixture into a freezer bag.
- Score the chicken breasts lightly with a sharp knife. This will help the marinade grab onto the chicken. Place the chicken in with the marinade. Secure the freezer bag before roughly shaking to help coat the chicken pieces.
- Leave in the fridge overnight or for at least 2–3 hours to help enhance the flavours.
- When you are ready to cook, tip the contents into a greased ovenproof dish.
- Cook for 20–30 minutes at 200°C until the chicken is cooked to your satisfaction.
- Serve on a bed of rice.

3 tablespoons olive oil
3 tablespoons natural Greek yoghurt (I use Total)
2 chillies
3–4 cloves garlic
2 teaspoons ground cinnamon
2 teaspoons paprika
2 teaspoons allspice
2–3 teaspoons runny honey
Zest and juice of 1 lime
Small handful of coriander leaves, finely chopped
Seasoning to taste
4–6 chicken breasts

Cooking rice

For those who are nervous about cooking rice, here are some simple tips. Choose your rice (basmati or long-grain is okay). I normally use 1½ times water to rice (you could measure this using a cup). Bring to the boil and simmer for 5 minutes. Pop on a lid and remove from the heat. Leave with the lid on for 10–15 minutes. Fluff up the rice using a fork before serving. I normally cook my rice with some frozen peas, chopped onions and peppers to add some extra variety. You can also add some flavours such as turmeric or pilau rice spices.

Lemon and Ginger Pork Chops

SERVES 4

60ml olive oil
½ bunch of spring onions, chopped
Juice and rind of 2 lemons
4cm knuckle fresh ginger, finely chopped
2 cloves garlic, crushed
Small handful of fresh coriander, finely chopped
200ml Greek yoghurt (I use Total as it holds whilst cooking)
Seasoning to taste
4 pork chops

You will need to marinate these, ideally for around 3–4 hours, to get a lovely moist and flavoursome chop. Once marinated, simply pop in the oven and cook for 20 minutes – so easy!

- Mix all the ingredients together apart from the chops.
- Add the chops, ensuring they are fully covered. You can either do this in the bowl you made the marinade in, or place the marinade in a freezer bag, add the chops and shake well to cover.
- Place the marinating chops in the fridge for at least 4 hours.
- Once ready to cook, place the chops in the base of an oiled ovenproof dish. Cover with the marinade.
- Place on the high rack and cook for 20 minutes at 190°C, or until the chops are cooked to your desired taste.
- Serve with a garnish of coriander leaves.

Spinach, Cheese and Ham Bake

A filling comfort supper!

- Place the spinach in a large colander over a large basin. Pour over boiling water until the leaves are wilted. Shake well and drain off all water.
- Line the bottom and sides of a heatproof dish with the slices of ham. Spread a thin layer of mustard over the ham. Then cover with the thinly sliced tomato, followed by a layer of the spinach and season to taste.
- Make some slight indents in the spinach for the eggs to sit in. Crack the eggs on top of the spinach. Depending on the size of your dish, you should get at least 4 eggs in.
- Drizzle the cream over the eggs evenly and finish with the cheese and finally the breadcrumbs. Season again.
- Place the dish on the high rack and bake at 200°C for 15 minutes until bubbling and brown.
- Serve with crusty bread.

SERVES 4

150g baby spinach
6–8 slices ham
1 teaspoon mustard
1–2 tomatoes, thinly sliced
Seasoning
4–6 free range eggs
4 tablespoons single cream
100g cheese, grated
50g breadcrumbs

Olive oil
50g butter
2 onions, finely
    chopped
2 cloves garlic, roughly
    chopped
150g mushrooms,
    chopped
125ml dry white wine
    or vermouth
Small handful of fresh
    thyme (or 1
    teaspoon dried)
4 chicken breasts
Freshly ground black
    pepper

Chicken and Wine Parcels

This is a really simple recipe which is very tasty. It can be prepared in advance.

- On the hob over a medium heat, melt a small knob of butter with a drizzle of olive oil in a sauté pan. Add the onion, garlic and mushrooms and cook until soft.
- Add the wine. Continue cooking for 5 minutes before adding the thyme.
- Place double-layered foil squares, big enough to parcel each chicken breast, on the worktop.
- Place a chicken breast in the centre of each piece of foil. Bring up the sides to form a bowl shape, as this will prevent the vegetable mixture from running off. Pour in 2 tablespoons of the vegetable mixture with each piece of chicken. Season and secure each parcel well. Then transfer to the high rack.
- Turn the halogen oven on to 200°C and cook for 25–30 minutes, until the chicken is tender.

Potato, Bacon and Spring Onion Frittata

Perfect for using up some leftovers – I always keep any leftover cooked potatoes wrapped in the fridge to use the next day for a frittata for a quick lunch or supper. Feel free to replace bacon with parma ham, pancetta or even chorizo sausage.

Olive oil
½ bunch of spring onions, finely chopped
4–6 rashers bacon, chopped
350g cooked potatoes, diced
4 eggs
30g mature cheese, grated
Seasoning

- On your hob, heat a drizzle of olive oil in an ovenproof/hobproof dish over a medium heat. (I have removed the handle from a heavy, non-stick frying pan and find this is now perfect for transferring food from the hob into the halogen.)
- Add the onion and bacon and cook for a few minutes before adding the potato. Cook until the potato is heated but not so much that it starts to stick.
- Beat the eggs, add the cheese and season. Pour this over the vegetables. Cook for 5 minutes to seal the base before placing on the high rack.
- Turn the temperature to 220°C and cook until firm and golden. This should take another 5–8 minutes. Serve immediately for a tasty quick lunch or supper.

4 chicken breasts,
   skinless
1 small tub garlic and
   herb low fat cream
   cheese
75g wholemeal
   breadcrumbs
50g oats
1 tablespoon fresh
   parsley, chopped
30g Parmesan cheese,
   grated
Seasoning
1 large egg, beaten

Healthy Chicken Kiev

Chicken Kiev can be incredibly tasty but also oozing with oil or butter. This is a really simple dish which gives you the same great taste but without the overpowering butter. You can make it in advance and even freeze it uncooked.

• Using a sharp knife, cut a pouch/pocket into each of your chicken breasts. Fill this pocket with the cream cheese – making sure you don't overfill as you don't want it bursting out when cooking.
• In a bowl, mix the breadcrumbs, oats, parsley and Parmesan. Season to taste.
• Brush each chicken breast with egg before dipping into the breadcrumbs mixture. Ensure it is evenly coated before placing on a greased baking tray.
• Once complete, turn the halogen on to 210°C and cook for 20–25 minutes until golden.
• Serve with a lovely salad and chunky chips!

One-pot Italian Lamb Steaks

SERVES 4

This is a really easy dish. You can prepare it in advance and leave in the fridge to marinate, or simply throw it together 30 minutes before you want to eat.

- Into your ovenproof dish, put all the ingredients apart from the lamb, and combine until evenly coated and distributed. Place the lamb in amongst the vegetables and press down until covered slightly with the juice. Place in the fridge, covered, until needed.
- When ready to cook, place on the high rack and set the halogen to 210°C. Cook for 20–30 minutes until the lamb is cooked to your satisfaction.
- Serve immediately with crusty bread and a green salad.

1 tin tomatoes
200ml red wine
100g cherry tomatoes
1 large red onion, cut into thick slices or wedges
1 red pepper, cut into thick slices
3–5 cloves garlic, left whole
100g black olives, halved
3–4 sprigs thyme,
Sea salt
Black pepper
4 lamb steaks

SERVES 4

Olive oil
1 onion, diced
3 cloves garlic,
  crushed
600g lamb, cubed
1 teaspoon ground
  cinnamon
1 teaspoon ground
  cardamom
1 teaspoon ground
  cloves
1 teaspoon curry
  powder
300ml plain Greek
  yoghurt
3 tomatoes, diced
250g long grain rice
Sprinkle of toasted
  almonds

Lamb Biryani

- In a sauté pan on your hob, heat a drizzle of oil over a medium/hot heat. Then add the lamb, onion and garlic and cook until the lamb starts to brown and the onion starts to soften.
- Add the spices and cook for a couple of minutes before adding the yoghurt and tomatoes. Combine well and cook gently on a low heat.
- Meanwhile cook your rice. I normally add 1½ water to rice, bring to the boil and leave simmering for 5 minutes. Then pop a lid on and remove completely from the heat. Leave to stand for 10–12 minutes. Fluff up using a fork.
- When the rice is done, place a layer in the bottom of your ovenproof dish. Follow this with a layer of the lamb mixture. Continue until you have used up all the ingredients.
- Cover with foil and place on the high rack. Turn the temperature to 180°C and cook for 15 minutes.
- Garnish with the toasted almonds before serving.

Spicy Lamb Kofta

- In a bowl, mix the lamb, onion, chilli, garlic, cumin, coriander, curry powder, ginger, half the coriander leaves and mango chutney. Combine well. Leave to rest for at least 2 hours.
- When ready to cook, scoop out small handfuls of the mixture and form into balls, approximately the size of a golf ball. (You can freeze these at this point. Simply place on a baking tray and pop in the freezer. Once frozen, you can place them into labelled freezer bags.)
- Fry in a little olive oil until they are brown and cooked through. Then transfer to an ovenproof dish.
- Pour over the curry sauce and sprinkle with freshly chopped coriander.
- Place on the high rack and set the temperature to 190°C. Cook for 20 minutes.
- Garnish with coriander. Serve with rice, mango chutney and naan bread.

500g lean lamb mince
1 onion, finely chopped
1 chilli, finely chopped
2–3 cloves garlic, crushed
1 teaspoon cumin
1 teaspoon ground coriander
2 teaspoons sweet curry powder
2cm knuckle fresh ginger, finely chopped
Small handful of fresh coriander leaves, chopped
3 tablespoons mango chutney
Olive oil
1 jar curry sauce (I use Rogan Josh)

Parma-wrapped Chilli Chicken

SERVES 4

2–3 tablespoons quark
  or low fat cream
  cheese
1 red chilli, finely
  chopped
1 teaspoon chilli
  powder
Few drops of Tabasco
  sauce to taste
  (optional)
Seasoning
4 chicken breasts
4–8 slices Parma ham
Olive oil

A very simple dish that takes minutes to prepare.

• Place the quark or cream cheese in a bowl and mix the chilli and Tabasco sauce until combined. Season to taste.
• Using a sharp knife, cut a slit in each chicken breast to form a pocket. Stuff the pockets with the creamed mixture.
• Wrap securely with Parma ham. Place seam-side down on a greased ovenproof dish. Drizzle with olive oil and season to taste.
• Place on the halogen's low rack and set the temperature to 200°C. Cook for 20–25 minutes until the chicken is cooked.

Balsamic Steaks

This is a really simple dish – just remember to marinate either overnight or for at least 2 hours before cooking.

- In a bowl, mix the sugar, garlic, chilli powder, paprika, balsamic vinegar, olive oil and seasoning together to form a paste.
- Dip the steaks into the mixture and leave coated overnight or for at least 2 hours before cooking.
- When ready to cook, set the halogen to 250°C. Place the steaks on the grill rack and grill on both sides until done to your desired taste.
- Serve with a green salad.

2 tablespoons brown sugar
3–4 garlic cloves, crushed
1–2 teaspoons mild/medium chilli powder
2 teaspoons paprika
3–4 tablespoons balsamic vinegar
2 tablespoons olive oil
Seasoning
4 lean steaks

SERVES 4

350g new potatoes,
    washed and halved
2 red onions, cut into
    wedges
3–4 cloves garlic,
    whole
1 red pepper, cut into
    wedges
12 cherry tomatoes
Olive oil
2–3 sprigs of thyme
4 chicken breasts
4–6 slices Parma ham
Paprika
Seasoning

Pan-roasted Vegetables and Chicken Breasts Wrapped in Parma Ham

A simple one-pot dish.

- Place the vegetables in an oiled ovenproof dish or roasting tin, making sure it fits well in your halogen oven. Drizzle with oil and add the sprigs of thyme. Toss well to ensure everything is evenly coated.
- Place on the high rack and set the temperature to 220°C. Cook for 10 minutes.
- Meanwhile, wrap the chicken breasts in the Parma ham.
- Remove the lid of the halogen and carefully (don't burn yourself) place the chicken breasts, seam-side down, into a gap in the vegetables. Sprinkle the chicken with paprika. Season to taste.
- Place the lid back on and cook at 200°C for 20–25 minutes, or until the chicken is cooked to your taste. If the vegetables start to brown too much, you can cover with foil, but the tomatoes and peppers go very sweet when they start to darken, and this can add to the flavour.
- Serve when the chicken is cooked to your satisfaction.

Garlic and Rosemary Chicken Parcels

A simple dish with great flavours that can be prepared in advance. Serve with sauté potatoes and steamed seasonal vegetables.

- Measure out 4 pieces of foil double the size of the chicken breasts. (You also may want to line this with parchment or you can buy from Lakeland parchment with a foil backing.) Brush the centre of each piece with olive oil.
- Place 1–2 slices of red onion on top of the olive oil. Place the chicken fillet on top of the onion. Season with the chicken seasoning. Repeat this for each parcel.
- In a small bowl or cup, mix the butter with the garlic. Place a spoonful of this butter mixture onto each of the chicken fillets. Sprinkle with the chopped rosemary and season to taste.
- Pull the sides of the foil up to form a bowl shape, ready to add the wine before scrunching securely. Once secure, place on your baking tray. You can leave to marinate until you are ready to cook, or cook immediately.
- Place on the high rack and set the halogen to 220°C. Cook for 10 minutes.
- Remove the lid of the halogen and very carefully unwrap the foil, exposing the chicken fillets but leaving the foil edges high to avoid the chicken juices from leaking. Cook for another 10–15 minutes or until the chicken is cooked to your satisfaction.
- Serve with sauté potatoes and steamed seasonal vegetables.

SERVES 4

Olive oil
4–8 slices red onion
4 chicken breasts
Chicken seasoning (I use Schwartz No Added Salt Chicken seasoning)
25g butter
3–4 cloves garlic, crushed
2 teaspoons fresh rosemary, chopped
Seasoning
100ml white wine or vermouth

4 chicken breasts
1 tablespoon olive oil
3 tablespoons cream cheese
1–2 tablespoons Dijon mustard
2–3 teaspoons chives, chopped
Sea salt
Black pepper

Chicken with Mustard Sauce

- Wash the chicken breasts, before cutting in half horizontally. Place on a sheet of greaseproof paper or clingfilm. With a rolling pin or meat mallet, flatten the chicken out until thin. Rub with olive oil.
- Mix the cream cheese with the mustard and chives and season to taste. Spread this mixture over the open chicken breasts.
- Carefully roll each breast up like a Swiss roll and secure with a wooden (ideally soaked) cocktail stick. Place on a greased browning tray.
- Turn the halogen oven on to 200°C and place the tray on the high rack. Cook for 15–20 minutes until cooked and golden.
- Serve with new potatoes and seasonal vegetables.

Fruity Chicken

- Into a deep ovenproof dish, put the olive oil and chicken breasts. Sprinkle the chicken with a dash of paprika.
- Place on the highest rack you can fit the dish into (this may be the high or grill rack depending on the height of your dish). Set the temperature to 220°C and brown the chicken on both sides.
- Once browned, add the onion and bacon and continue to cook for another 5–8 minutes until the onion and bacon start to soften.
- Add the remaining ingredients and season with sea salt and black pepper.
- Cover with a lid or double layer of tin foil and turn the temperature down to 180°C. Cook for another 20–25 minutes.
- Serve with fluffy mashed potato and seasonal vegetables.

Olive oil
4 chicken breasts
Dash of paprika
1 red onion, chopped
3–4 thick rashers
   smoked bacon or
   lardons, thickly
   diced
8 no-soak prunes,
   chopped roughly
8 no-soak apricots,
   chopped roughly
1 teaspoon fresh
   rosemary, chopped
300ml chicken stock
100ml white wine
Black pepper
Sea salt

Beefy Stuffed Onions with Goat's Cheese Topping

SERVES 4

4 large onions, peeled
Knob of butter
Olive oil
350g lean minced beef
4 tomatoes, finely
   chopped
2 tablespoons tomato
   purée
100ml red wine
   (optional)
3 cloves garlic,
   crushed
1–2 sprigs of thyme
1 teaspoon fresh
   rosemary, chopped
Sea salt
Black pepper
100g goat's cheese

This is a lovely dish which is also very filling. If you are vegetarian you can opt to use veggie or Quorn mince instead of the beef. These can be prepared in advance and reheated.

- Boil the onions in a pan of water for 5 minutes. Drain and leave until cool enough to handle.
- Cut off the top of each onion and remove the inside, leaving a thick outer shell. Chop the discarded onion and leave to one side as you will need this later. Spread the butter inside the onion shells and place into a greased ovenproof dish.
- Heat the olive oil in a sauté pan and cook the chopped onion until it softens. Add the mince and continue to cook until it has browned. Once browned, add the chopped tomatoes, tomato purée, red wine (optional), garlic, thyme, rosemary and seasoning. Cook for another couple of minutes until thoroughly combined and heated through.
- Spoon the mixture into the onion shells. Finish with a thick layer of goat's cheese, followed by a sprinkle of black pepper.
- Place on the high rack at 190°C and bake for 20–25 minutes until the onion is soft and the goat's cheese is golden and bubbling.
- Serve with a lovely green salad.

Chicken, Mushroom and Bacon Lasagna

Ideal for using up any cooked chicken. As with all lasagne cooked in the halogen, you can speed up the cooking process by using fresh lasagna sheets or parboil before adding to the dish.

- Place the olive oil into a sauté pan and cook the mushrooms and bacon for 5–8 minutes. Remove from the heat.
- Melt the butter in a heavy-based saucepan. Add the flour and stir well with a wooden spoon. Gradually add the milk and bring slowly to the boil, stirring all the time. You may want to add more milk if you think it is too little.
- Add the chicken, mushrooms and bacon to the sauce. Stir well, before seasoning with sea salt and black pepper.
- In another bowl, combine the tomatoes, herbs and seasoning together.
- Start to layer your lasagna by placing some of the tomato mixture in the base of an ovenproof dish, followed by lasagna sheets, followed by the chicken mixture. Continue, finishing with lasagna sheets on the top.
- Mix together the yoghurt and the egg and spread over the top. Sprinkle with the Parmesan cheese and season with black pepper.
- Place the lasagna on the high rack. Turn the temperature to 200°C and cook for approximately 40 minutes (shorter if you have parboiled the lasagna sheets or used fresh). If it starts to darken on top, cover securely with tin foil.
- Serve with potato wedges and green salad.

SERVES 4

Olive oil

200g mushrooms, sliced (mixture of types is good)

8 rashers lean bacon, diced

Knob of butter

1 tablespoon plain flour or cornflour

350ml milk

250g cooked chicken, chopped

Sea salt

Black pepper

400g tinned tomatoes, drained and chopped

1 teaspoon dried mixed herbs

Lasagna sheets

250ml Greek yoghurt

1 beaten egg

1–2 tablespoons Parmesan cheese, grated

1 bulb garlic, peeled
200ml olive oil
Juice and zest of 1
    lemon
1–2 tablespoons crème
    fraîche
1 teaspoon mustard
Black pepper
Sea salt
4 chicken breasts
    (depending on
    appetite!)

Garlicky Chicken

This really is garlicky, so if you don't like garlic, avoid this dish. You can use whatever chicken pieces you prefer – I favour chicken breasts. Prepare up to a day in advance as this allows the flavours to really develop.

- Using a food processor or electric mini chopping gadget, whizz the garlic cloves, olive oil, lemon juice and zest until they form a smooth creamy paste. Add the crème fraîche and mustard, before seasoning with black pepper and sea salt.
- Wash the chicken pieces and place them in a greased ovenproof dish, just big enough to hold the chicken. Pour over the sauce, ensuring the chicken is well covered.
- Cover with a double layer of tin foil and place in the fridge to marinate overnight or for at least 2 hours.
- Just before you are ready to cook, remove from the fridge and bring to room temperature. Then place (with foil still intact) on the high rack and cook at 200°C for 25–30 minutes until the chicken is tender and cooked to your requirements.
- Serve with green vegetables and mini roast potatoes.

Tender Chilli Chicken in Breadcrumbs

This is a really lovely dish, made all the better by marinating for at least an hour, or overnight, before adding the breadcrumbs. Remember to stock your freezer with breadcrumbs made from any stale bread you have lurking in your bread bin. Bag in freezer bags ready for toppings, coatings or even an indulgent treacle tart!

- Flatten your chicken breasts using a rolling pin or wooden kitchen mallet. You need to get them as thin as possible.
- Place the olive oil, white wine, garlic, chilli, lemon juice and seasoning in your food processor and whizz until smooth. Pour over the chicken, cover with foil or clingfilm and place in the fridge to marinate for at least 2 hours.
- When you are ready to cook the chicken, remove from the fridge so it reaches room temperature before cooking. While you are waiting, place the remaining ingredients in a bowl and combine well.
- Sprinkle the breadcrumbs mix over the chicken pieces, pressing down well where you can.
- Place on the high rack and set the temperature at 200°C. Cook for 15–20 minutes.
- Serve with a lovely crisp green salad and for an extra chilli hit, some sweet chilli sauce.

4 chicken fillets
2 tablespoons olive oil
2–3 tablespoons white wine or vermouth
2–3 cloves garlic
1 red chilli
Juice of 1 lemon
Sea salt
Black pepper
100g fresh breadcrumbs
Pinch of dried thyme
Pinch of cayenne pepper
40g Parmesan, grated

Spicy Polenta Chicken

SERVES 4

2 teaspoons coriander
  seeds
1 red chilli, finely
  chopped
2–3 cloves garlic, finely
  chopped
1–2 teaspoons sweet
  curry powder
500g ready-to-use
  polenta
1 large red onion, cut
  into wedges
8–12 cherry tomatoes,
  whole
Handful of coriander
  leaves
4 boneless chicken
  breasts
4 tablespoons natural
  Greek yoghurt
Black pepper
Sea salt
Olive oil

I had never cooked with polenta until I found a recipe using Italian flavours. Polenta can be a bit tasteless so I would advise, if you like your flavours, to season well and use some spices. I love the flavour of coriander seeds and, just as with sweet potatoes, they work really well with polenta.

• Using a pestle and mortar, grind the coriander seeds. Add half the chopped chilli, the garlic and the sweet curry powder and combine well.
• In a roasting dish or deep baking tray, crumble the polenta into bite-sized chunks. Spread evenly around the base of the dish. Sprinkle the spice mixture evenly over the polenta. Finish by placing the onion, tomatoes and a few coriander leaves in amongst the polenta.
• Use a sharp knife to slash the top of the chicken breasts gently – 3 or 4 lines will be perfect. Place the chicken in the dish with the polenta. Carefully place the Greek yoghurt over the top of the chicken to form a coating.
• Season the whole dish with black pepper, sea salt and the remaining chopped chilli. Finish with a generous drizzle of olive oil.
• Place the dish on the high rack and set the temperature to 220°C. Cook for 20–30 minutes until the chicken is golden. Serve immediately.

Grilled Pepper Chicken Salad

- Cut the chicken breasts into thick strips.
- Mix the lemon zest, juice, garlic and black peppercorns together.
- Place the chicken in a freezer bag. Add the lemon juice mixture and shake well. Leave to marinate overnight or for at least 1 hour.
- When ready to serve, remove the chicken and place on the grill rack (see the Grilling section in Chapter 1 for tips). Set the temperature to 250°C and cook for 5 minutes, then turn and cook again until the chicken is thoroughly cooked.
- Meanwhile, place the salad leaves in a large serving dish. Add the onion and cherry tomatoes. Combine well and dress.
- Place the cooked chicken on the salad. Serve immediately.

4 chicken breasts, skinless
Zest and juice of 1 lemon
2–3 cloves garlic, crushed
2–3 teaspoons black peppercorns, crushed
100g salad leaves, washed
1 red onion, sliced
12–16 cherry tomatoes, halved
Salad dressing of your choice

Stuffed Spicy Lamb Courgettes

2–4 courgettes

Seasoning

Olive oil

1 onion, finely chopped

2 cloves garlic, crushed

½ –1 chilli, finely crushed

1–2 teaspoons curry powder

1 teaspoon cumin

1 teaspoon dried mint

½ teaspoon ground cinnamon

250g minced lamb

½ tin chopped tomatoes

30g sultanas

This is also a great dish if you have any left over bolognese from a previous meal. Simply add some spices to zing it up or serve as a tomato and herb bolognese topped with parmesan.

- Cut the courgettes in half lengthways. Using a teaspoon, gently scoop out the soft flesh, retaining this for later. You should be left with approximately 2–3mm of flesh around the edges of the courgette.
- Place the courgettes on a baking tray. Season and drizzle with a little olive oil. Place on the high rack and cook for 15 minutes at 180°C.
- Meanwhile, pour some olive oil into a large sauté pan and add the onion, garlic and chilli. Cook on your hob over a medium/hot heat for a few minutes to help soften before adding the herbs and spices, followed by the lamb.
- When the lamb has browned, add the chopped tomatoes and sultanas. You may want to add a little water or stock if it starts to dry out a little. Season to taste.
- When the courgettes have started to soften, remove the tray from the halogen. Carefully spoon the mince mixture into the courgettes.
- Place them back into the halogen and continue to cook at 180°C for another 10–15 minutes.
- Serve immediately.

Rump Steak with Red Wine and Rosemary Sauce

A simple dish that can be prepared in advance, leaving you time to enjoy your day. Simply grill and heat the sauce when ready.

- In a sauté pan or saucepan, heat the butter on a gentle heat. Add the garlic and cook gently until the flavour of the garlic starts to waft around the kitchen. Don't let it burn!
- Add the red wine, rosemary and tomato purée and cook for 5 minutes. Leave aside until you are almost ready to serve.
- Prepare your steaks for grilling and season to taste. Place on the grill rack and turn the temperature to 250°C (see the Grilling section in Chapter 1 for tips).
- Cook the steaks to your requirements. (I usually cook for 7–8 minutes each side but much depends on the height of the racks, the thickness of steaks and really how well you like them cooked.)
- Meanwhile, reheat the sauce gently, bringing it to a boil to help thicken slightly before serving.
- Remove the steaks from the oven and pour over the sauce. Serve with mashed potato and green vegetables.

SERVES 2

15g butter
2–3 cloves garlic, crushed
150ml red wine
2–3 sprigs of rosemary
1 teaspoon tomato purée
2 rump steaks
Seasoning

500g chicken fillets, diced

2–3 tablespoons tikka masala paste

Cheat's Chicken Tikka Kebabs

This is so easy it is almost embarrassing to include it as a recipe, but oh so popular! Remember, if you are using wooden skewers, you will first need to soak them for a few hours.

• Dice the chicken fillets evenly. Place in a bowl along with the tikka masala paste. Combine well, ensuring the chicken is evenly coated.

• Cover with clingfilm and place in the fridge for at least an hour.

• When ready to cook, remove from the fridge and thread the chicken onto your soaked wooden skewers (or metal skewers).

• Turn the halogen oven to the highest setting, place the kebabs on the grill rack and cook, turning regularly, for 15–20 minutes, or until the chicken is done to your satisfaction. (See the Grilling section in Chapter 1 for tips.)

• Serve on a bed of rice for a delicious yet simple meal.

Turkey with Pesto

This is a really easy meal but tastes divine.

- Rub the turkey with olive oil and place on a baking tray.
- Carefully spoon pesto over each of the turkey fillets. Season with black pepper.
- Place on the high rack and cook for 20–25 minutes, or until the turkey is cooked to your requirements.
- Serve with mini roast potatoes and green vegetables.

SERVES 4

4 turkey fillets
Olive oil
Green pesto
Black pepper

Garlic and Mustard Roast Leg of Lamb

SERVES 4–6

1 leg of lamb
Olive oil
3–4 tablespoons
   mustard powder
8–10 cloves garlic,
   crushed
2–3 sprigs of rosemary
Seasoning
6–8 potatoes
1–2 tablespoons
   paprika
2–3 tablespoons
   semolina

- Rub olive oil over the leg of lamb. Follow this with the mustard powder, rubbing well to ensure it is evenly coated. Using a sharp knife, make little inserts and push in the garlic cloves and rosemary sprigs. Then season to taste.
- Place on the low rack and cook for 15 minutes at 230°C.
- Meanwhile, peel and quarter the potatoes and steam or parboil for 10 minutes. Drain and return to the empty saucepan.
- Add the paprika and semolina. Pop the lid back on the saucepan and shake to fluff up and coat the potatoes. Then place them around the lamb and brush with olive oil.
- Cook for another 10 minutes before turning down to 190°C and cooking for a further 30–45 minutes or until both the meat and potatoes are cooked to your satisfaction. Timings for lamb depend on the size of the joint. Throughout, remember to turn the lamb and potatoes regularly and add a brush of oil as required.
- Serve with steamed vegetables and homemade gravy.

Lamb Steaks with Mediterranean Vegetables

- Into a large ovenproof dish, put all the vegetables. Combine well. Then place the sprigs of rosemary in amongst the vegetables.
- Drizzle with olive oil, a sprinkle of sea salt, a tiny sprinkle of sugar and a light drizzle of balsamic vinegar (not too much or you will overpower the dish).
- Place on the high rack and set the temperature to 190°C. Cook for 30 minutes.
- Remove and add the olives and a little more oil if needed. Pop back in the oven for another 10 minutes.
- Brush the lamb steaks with a little garlic oil. Season to taste.
- Remove the vegetables and place them on the base of the halogen oven. Put the grill rack in the halogen as you are going to grill the lamb steaks. You may need to improvise to get the rack high – I normally put a tray onto the ovenproof dish and pop the rack onto the tray (see the Grilling section in Chapter 1 for tips).
- Turn the temperature to 250°C and place your steaks on the grill rack. Grill each side for approximately 5–8 minutes. (This depends on how close the steaks are to the heat and also to your own taste – just program and test every few minutes.)
- To serve, place the steaks on the plate and spoon over the vegetables.

2 red onions, cut into wedges
½ bulb garlic, left whole and unpeeled
2 courgettes, thickly sliced
2 red peppers, thickly sliced
½ aubergine, thickly sliced
2 sweet potatoes, unpeeled and sliced
12 cherry tomatoes
3 sprigs of rosemary
Olive oil
Sea salt
Sugar
Balsamic vinegar
Handful of olives
4 lamb steaks
Garlic oil

Hot and Sticky Chicken Drumsticks

SERVES 4

4–6 chicken
  drumsticks
2 tablespoons runny
  clear honey
2 tablespoons
  Worcester sauce
2 tablespoons tomato
  sauce
1 tablespoon paprika
1 chilli, finely
  chopped
1 teaspoon chilli
  powder
½ teaspoon cayenne
  pepper
Seasoning

- Score the chicken drumsticks with a sharp knife.
- In a bowl, mix the remaining ingredients and season to taste.
- Place the drumsticks in the marinade and leave for at least 2 hours, ideally overnight.
- When ready to cook, turn the halogen to 250°C. Place a baking tray on the grill rack (see the Grilling section in Chapter 1 for tips).
- Grill the drumsticks on each side until cooked. Times can depend on the machine used as the height of the grill rack varies, but it should take approximately 10 minutes each side. Check the chicken is cooked through before serving.
- Serve hot or cold on a bed of rice with a lovely salad.

Smoky Bacon, Chicken and Tomato Kebabs

SERVES 4

- Cut the bacon lengthways and thread one end onto the skewer, using metal skewers or wooden if they are pre-soaked.
- Put a piece of chicken next to the bacon and then secure the bacon back onto the skewer so it covers one side of the chicken. Thread again with a tomato, and if you have some bacon left dangling, thread this again. Finish with a slice of pepper.
- Repeat with the chicken and bacon combination until you reach the end of the skewer.
- Turn the halogen oven to 250°C and place the kebabs on the grill rack (see the Grilling section in Chapter 1 for tips).
- Cook, turning regularly, for 15–20 minutes or until the chicken is done to your satisfaction.
- Serve on a bed of rice for a delicious yet simple meal.

16 rashers smoky
  bacon
300g chicken pieces
12–16 cherry tomatoes
1–2 red peppers,
  thickly sliced

Zesty Honeyed Chicken with Wild Rocket

SERVES 4

4 chicken breasts
2 tablespoons runny honey
Zest and juice of 1 lemon
Zest and juice of ½ lime
Zest and juice of ½ orange
Black pepper
Sea salt
Olive oil
100g wild rocket

- Score the top of the chicken breasts with a sharp knife as this gives the sauce something to hang on to.
- In a bowl, mix the honey, lemon, lime and orange zest and juice. Combine well. Season to taste.
- Pour a little olive oil into your baking tray and add the chicken.
- Using a pastry brush, brush the honey mixture onto the top of the chicken breasts, ensuring they are evenly coated.
- Place on the high rack and set the temperature to 200°C.
- Cook for 20–25 minutes until the chicken is cooked through.
- Serve immediately on a bed of wild rocket.

Garlic and Ginger Pork Steaks

SERVES 4

- Place the pork steaks into a greased ovenproof dish.
- Combine the garlic paste with the ginger and season with black pepper.
- Spread the paste onto the top of the pork steaks. Cover the dish with clingfilm and leave to marinate in the fridge overnight or all day.
- When you are ready to cook, remove the clingfilm and place the steaks on the high rack.
- Set the temperature to 200°C and cook for 20 minutes or to your requirements.
- Serve with sweet potato mash and green vegetables.

4–8 pork steaks
3–4 teaspoons garlic paste (or crush 4–6 cloves garlic and mix with a little olive oil)
3cm knuckle of ginger, finely chopped
Black pepper

Curried Chicken Drumsticks

2 tablespoons chilli
   olive oil
Zest and juice of ½
   lemon
1 small onion
1 chilli, finely
   chopped
3 cloves garlic
2cm knuckle of ginger
1 teaspoon turmeric
1 teaspoon cumin
2 teaspoons curry
   powder
3 tomatoes
Small handful of
   coriander
3 tablespoons water
Black pepper
Sea salt
6–8 chicken
   drumsticks

- Place all the ingredients apart from the chicken drumsticks in a food processor and whizz to form a paste.
- Place the chicken drumsticks in a greased ovenproof dish. Pour over the sauce, cover with foil and leave in the fridge for at least 2 hours or overnight.
- When ready to cook, simply place on the medium rack with the foil still intact.
- Set the temperature to 200°C and cook for 20 minutes. Remove the foil, add a few more tablespoons of water if the sauce appears too dry, and cook again for another 10–15 minutes or until the chicken is cooked through.
- Serve on a bed of rice.

Wholegrain Mustard Steak Salad

SERVES 4

- Place the steaks on the grill rack (see the section on Grilling in Chapter 1 for tips) and set the temperature to 250°C. Grill on one side for approximately 4–5 minutes.
- Turn over and coat the top of each steak with wholegrain mustard, as thick as you desire. Continue to grill for another 4–5 minutes. (The grilling time can vary depending on the height of your rack and also the thickness of the steaks – adjust to suit your own requirements.)
- Remove from the oven and wrap the steaks in foil. Leave to rest while you prepare the salad.
- In a serving dish, place the salad leaves, onion and cherry tomatoes.
- In a jug, mix the olive oil and vinegar and season to taste. Taste and add more vinegar or olive oil to suit your own palate.
- Toss the salad leaves with your dressing.
- Unwrap the steaks and thickly slice. Place the slices of steak on top of the salad, toss again and serve immediately.

2–3 fillet steaks
Approx. 3 tablespoons wholegrain mustard
1 bag peppery mixed leaf salad (watercress, rocket, etc.) washed
1 red onion, finely sliced
12–16 cherry tomatoes, halved
2 tablespoons olive oil
1–2 tablespoons white wine vinegar
Seasoning

750g new potatoes
Small handful of fresh
    mint leaves
4–6 eggs
1 pack lean bacon
75g salad leaves
½ bunch of spring
    onions
12–16 cherry
    tomatoes, halved
½ cucumber
1–2 teaspoons chives,
    chopped
2 tablespoons olive oil
1 tablespoon white
    wine vinegar
1 teaspoon wholegrain
    mustard
Seasoning

Bacon and Egg Salad

A burst of flavours for a delicious and simple salad.

- Cook the potatoes (boil or steam) with a little fresh mint.
- Meanwhile, hard-boil the eggs.
- Put the bacon on the browning tray and place on the grill rack (see the Grilling section in Chapter 1 for tips). Set the temperature to 250°C.
- Cook until the bacon is crispy – this should take around 5–7 minutes but timing depends on the height of your rack.
- Place the salad leaves, spring onions, cherry tomatoes and cucumber in a large serving dish. Add the remaining mint and chives. Combine well.
- In a jug, mix the olive oil, vinegar and wholegrain mustard. Combine well and season to taste. Add more vinegar or olive oil to suit your own palate.
- Drain the potatoes when cooked and place in the serving dish.
- Chop the bacon and add to the salad. Finally shell your eggs and halve or quarter them and place on the top of the salad.
- Add the salad dressing to taste. Serve immediately.

Bacon, Sausage and Potato Hash

Perfect with some fried eggs served alongside!

- Boil or steam the potato chunks until they are just starting to soften – don't overcook! Then drain and place on an oiled baking tray.
- Add the sausages, bacon and onion.
- Sprinkle with paprika and season with black pepper and sea salt. Drizzle with a little olive oil.
- Set your halogen to 210°C. Place on the high rack and cook for 20–30 minutes, or until the sausages, bacon and potatoes are cooked and crispy. It may help to toss the contents halfway through the cooking time, to ensure everything is evenly cooked and crisp.
- Serve immediately for a tasty supper or brunch.

SERVES 4–6

3–4 large potatoes, cut into 2–3cm chunks
Olive oil
6–8 lean sausages, cut into thick slices
1 pack lean thick bacon, cut into thick chunks
1 large onion, chopped
Sprinkle of paprika
Black pepper
Sea salt

125g lean bacon
100g peppery salad
  leaves (watercress,
  rocket, etc.), washed
½ bunch of spring
  onions, finely
  chopped
175g peas (fresh or
  defrosted frozen)
75g sugarsnap peas,
  roughly chopped
Salad dressing
Seasoning

Bacon and Pea Salad

- Place the bacon on the high rack as you are going to grill it (see the Grilling section in Chapter 1 for tips). Set the temperature to 250°C and cook for 4–5 minutes each side or until crispy.
- Meanwhile, place the salad leaves in a large serving dish. Add the spring onions, peas and sugarsnap peas. Combine well.
- Remove the bacon and roughly chop. Combine with the salad leaves.
- Drizzle with salad dressing and season. Serve immediately.

Chicken and Mushroom Pancake Bake

This is a really lovely meal. You can use readymade pancakes or make your own – see the recipe on page 140.

- Heat some olive oil in a sauté pan on your hob. Add the onion, garlic, celery and mushrooms and cook over a medium/hot heat until they just start to soften.
- Add the cooked chicken and cook for another couple of minutes before adding the cream cheese, milk, tarragon and black pepper. Remove from the heat.
- Lay out your pancakes one at a time. Pop a line of the mixture across one side of the pancake and roll into a sausage. Place each rolled pancake in a greased ovenproof dish.
- Pour over the sauce and finish with the grated parmesan.
- Place in the halogen oven on the high rack. Set the temperature to 200°C and cook for 25 minutes.
- Serve with a lovely green salad and new, minted potatoes.

SERVES 4

Olive oil
1 onion, finely
  chopped
2 cloves garlic,
  crushed (optional)
2 sticks of celery, finely
  chopped
80g button
  mushrooms, halved
300g chicken, cooked
  and chopped
300g cream cheese
100ml milk
½ teaspoon dried
  tarragon
Black pepper
6–8 pancakes
  (depending on size
  of ovenproof dish)
1 jar tomato pasta
  sauce
30g Parmesan cheese,
  grated

4 potatoes
2 sweet potatoes
1 carrot
Seasoning
2 tablespoons butter
2 tablespoons plain
  flour
300ml chicken stock
100ml white wine
3–4 tablespoons single
  cream
½ teaspoon dried
  tarragon (or a few
  sprigs of fresh, finely
  chopped)
Black pepper
Olive oil
1 onion, finely
  chopped
400g pheasant, cooked
  and chopped
125g chestnut
  mushrooms,
  quartered

Golden Pheasant and Mushroom Bake

A lovely, creamy, pheasant and mushroom base topped with a golden mash.

- Chop the potato, sweet potato and carrot into chunks. Boil or steam until soft. Drain and mash with a little butter and season to taste.
- Whilst the vegetables are cooking you can prepare the rest of the dish. In a saucepan on your hob, melt the butter over a medium/hot heat. Add the flour and stir for a few seconds to form a paste.
- Gradually add the chicken stock and white wine and keep stirring to form a sauce. Add the cream. If the sauce starts to go lumpy, use a balloon whisk and beat well. Cook until it thickens.
- Add the tarragon and black pepper. Leave to one side.
- Heat some olive oil in a sauté pan over a medium/hot heat. Add the onion, cooked pheasant and the chestnut mushrooms. Cook until the mushrooms start to soften. Add the sauce. Heat through and pour into a deep, ovenproof dish.
- Place the mashed mixture onto the pheasant base. Using a fork, level out the top.
- When you are ready to cook, place on the low rack and set the temperature to 200°C. Cook for 20–25 minutes until the potato is golden.
- Serve with green vegetables.

Macaroni Bolognese Bake

SERVES 4

- On the hob, fry the onion and garlic in a little olive oil until soft and translucent. Add the pepper if using one. Add the mince and cook until brown, followed by the wine and mushrooms, tomatoes or cheat pasta sauce and cook for 10 minutes. Finally, add the herbs and season to taste. Leave to simmer for 10 minutes.
- While the bolognese mix is simmering, place the macaroni in a pan of boiling water and cook as manufactures instructions. Meanwhile, make the white sauce.
- Melt the butter gently in a saucepan on a medium heat (not high!). Add the flour of cornflour and stir well with a wooden spoon. Add the milk, a little at a time, continuing to stir to avoid lumps.
- Switch now to a balloon whisk. Continue to stir over a medium heat until the sauce begins to thicken. The balloon whisk will also help eradicate any lumps that may have formed. Add more milk as necessary to get the desired thickness. The sauce should be the thickness of custard. Add mustard and season with black pepper.
- Drain the macaroni and add half the white sauce and a beaten egg. Stir well.
- Place a layer of the macaroni in the base of your ovenproof dish. Add a layer of the bolognese mixture and repeat. Finish with the remaining sauce and the grated cheese.
- Place on the low rack, at 190° and cook for 15–20 minutes.
- Serve with green salad.

1 onion, finely chopped
2–3 cloves garlic, finely chopped
A spray of olive oil
1 pepper, finely chopped (optional)
400g lean beef mince or, for vegetarians, veggie mince
150ml red wine
75g mushrooms, finely chopped (optional)
3–4 fresh tomatoes, chopped, or 1 tin chopped tomatoes
mixed herbs to taste
seasoning to taste

For the white sauce
25g butter
1 tablespoon plain flour or cornflour
500–750ml milk
¼ teaspoon mustard (optional)
Black pepper to taste

200g macaroni
1 egg, beaten
750g grated mature cheese

Fish

As a nutritionist, I encourage people to eat more fish than red meat, especially fish rich in omega-3 such as mackerel, trout, sardines, tuna and salmon. As with meat, make sure the fish is cooked right through – too high a heat and it can burn on the outside and remain raw in the middle.

There are many recipes in this chapter that involve parcelling the food for cooking. Remember to secure the foil parcel well but allow some room for expansion during cooking. Remember that the foil and contents can be extremely hot when you are ready to serve, so take care not to burn yourself, especially with the escaping steam.

Golden Oat Crunch Fish Fingers

300g white fish fillets
   (such as cod or
   pollock)
100g wholemeal
   breadcrumbs
50g oats
1 carrot, grated
Seasoning
1 large egg, beaten

These fish fingers are simple to make and can be frozen. They are perfect for children – get away from the yucky processed fish fingers and encourage them into the healthier option.

- Cut your fish fillets into thick fingers.
- In a bowl, mix the breadcrumbs, oats and carrot, and season to taste.
- Brush each fish finger with egg before dipping into the breadcrumbs mixture, ensuring they are well covered. Place the fingers onto a greased baking tray. You can either freeze them until needed or bake immediately.
- Preheat your halogen oven to 210°C. Place the tray on the high rack and bake for 15 minutes, turning once.
- Serve with chunky chips and mushy peas.

Baked Trout with Creamy Lemon and Dill Sauce

SERVES 4

- Rub the fillets with olive oil and season with black pepper.
- Place each fillet on its own sheet of aluminium foil large enough to parcel up the fillet. (You may also want to line the foil with parchment or you can buy from Lakeland parchment with a foil backing.)
- Place the garlic, chilli and pepper on the fish.
- Mix the lemon juice (to taste), dill and yoghurt together. Season to taste. Place 1–2 dessertspoons on each fillet.
- Fold the foil up to form a secure parcel and place on the high rack. Set the temperature to 200°C and bake for 15–20 minutes.
- Serve with new potatoes and fresh seasonal greens.

4 rainbow trout fillets
Olive oil
Black pepper
2–4 cloves garlic, sliced
1 chilli, diced
1 pepper, diced (any colour but red looks the most attractive)
Lemon juice
Small handful of fresh dill, chopped
4–8 dessertspoons natural yoghurt
Seasoning

Coley, Tomato and Red Pepper Kebabs

SERVES 4

4–5 tablespoons natural yoghurt

Small handful of fresh mint, finely chopped

Zest and juice of ½ lime

Black pepper

3–4 coley fillets, skinned

Bay leaves

12–16 cherry tomatoes

2–3 red peppers, cut into thick chunks

You can use any fish for these kebabs – I use coley as it is a family favourite and cheap to buy, but feel free to experiment. If you are using wooden skewers, remember to soak them overnight before use or they will burn. Metal skewers obviously are easier, but be careful as they get very hot.

- In a bowl mix the yoghurt, mint and lime together. Season with black pepper.
- Cut the fish fillets into chunks. Holding the skewers, carefully thread the fish, bay leaf, cherry tomato and pepper, repeating until the skewers are filled.
- Using a pastry brush, brush the cod with the yoghurt mixture, ensuring it is evenly coated.
- Turn the halogen to 250°C. Place the skewers on your grilling rack (see the section on Grilling in Chapter 1 for tips).
- Cook for 8–10 minutes, or until the fish is cooked to your taste, turning frequently to ensure the kebabs are evenly cooked. Note that the grilling time also depends on how close to the heat the kebabs are, as this can vary according to the machine and equipment used.
- Serve immediately on a bed of fragrant rice.

Honeyed Salmon and Asparagus Parcels

My mum passed on this recipe which is truly delicious and so simple. Yes, it is another parcel recipe but really, why not? They are so simple and save on washing up – what's not to like? Try to buy the asparagus when in season – the taste of fresh British asparagus is second to none.

- Mix the melted butter, honey, mustard and lemon zest together. Season to taste.
- Prepare 4 squares of foil, big enough to parcel the fish. (You may also want to line this with parchment or you can buy from Lakeland parchment with a foil backing.)
- Place the asparagus on each of the tin foil squares, followed by the salmon fillets. Drizzle with the honey mixture. Seal the foil parcels securely.
- Turn the halogen oven to 210°C. Place the parcels on the middle rack. Cook for 20–25 minutes or until the fish flakes easily.
- Serve with new potatoes and green seasonal vegetables.

SERVES 4

20g butter, melted
3 tablespoons runny honey
1 tablespoon Dijon mustard
Zest of ½ lemon
Seasoning
250g fresh asparagus, trimmed
4 salmon fillets

4 salmon fillets
100ml white wine or
  vermouth
Zest and juice of 1
  lemon
Black pepper
4 tablespoons pesto
2 tablespoons
  wholemeal
  breadcrumbs

Easy Pesto Salmon

This really is a simple dish. Try to remember to marinate before cooking for at least 1 hour, but ideally 3–4 hours as this really improves the flavour.

- Place the salmon fillets in a freezer bag. Add the white wine and lemon zest and juice. Season to taste with black pepper. Seal, shake well and leave in the fridge to marinate.
- When you are ready to cook, turn the halogen to high (240–250°C) as you are going to grill the salmon (see the section on Grilling in Chapter 1 for tips).
- Remove the salmon from the bag and place on a greased baking tray. Spread the pesto over the top of each fillet. Finish with a sprinkle of fresh breadcrumbs.
- Place on the grilling rack and cook for 10 minutes or until the fish is done to your requirements. You should be able to flake the fish with a fork. Note that the cooking time also depends on how close to the heat the salmon is, as this can vary according to the machine and equipment used.
- Serve immediately.

Spicy Cod

This is really simple but tastes amazing. You can make the paste in advance and store in the fridge ready to use.

- Into a food processor put all the ingredients apart from the cod. Blend until a smooth paste is formed. If it is too dry add a dash of olive oil and some more lime juice. (If your lime seems reluctant to give up any juice, heat it gently for a minute or two before juicing.)
- Wash the cod and place in a greased ovenproof dish. Carefully place the paste on the top of the cod, ensuring it is evenly coated. Cover with clingfilm and leave in the fridge for at least 30 minutes.
- When you are ready to cook, remove the clingfilm and place on the high rack. Set the temperature to 190°C and cook for 15–20 minutes until the fish is cooked.
- Serve with a lovely herb and green leaf salad.

SERVES 4

2–3 tablespoons olive oil
½–1 chilli, seeded
2–3 cloves garlic
2cm piece of fresh ginger
½ teaspoon turmeric
1–2 teaspoons sweet curry powder
Small handful of fresh coriander
Small handful of fresh mint
Zest and juice of 1 lime
4 cod fillets, skinned

2 red peppers, diced
½ cucumber, diced
1 red onion, diced
3 tomatoes, diced
1 chilli, diced
2–3 cloves garlic,
    crushed
Small handful of flat
    leaf parsley, chopped
1 dessertspoonful
    balsamic vinegar
Olive oil
Black pepper
Lemon juice
4 tuna steaks

Tuna Steak with Spicy Salsa

A delicious meal served on its own or with asparagus and new potatoes.

- Into a bowl, put the chopped vegetables, spices, parsley, balsamic vinegar, 3 tablespoons of olive oil and season with black pepper. Combine well.
- Rub olive oil into the tuna steaks. Drizzle with lemon juice and season with black pepper.
- Turn the halogen on to 250°C and place the steaks on the grilling rack (see the section on Grilling in Chapter 1 for tips).
- Cook for approximately 3–4 minutes each side, or until done to your desired taste. Note that the timing may need to be adjusted according to the thickness of your steaks and also on how close to the heat the steaks are, as this can vary according to the machine and equipment used.
- Once cooked, place on your plates and spoon on the salsa.
- Serve with asparagus and new potatoes.

Italian-style Grilled Coley

SERVES 4

This uses one of my favourite sauces made in the halogen. I like to make this sauce in a large batch and keep it in my fridge – perfect for pasta dishes, mixed with some beans or, as in this recipe, to top some grilled fish.

- In a deep ovenproof dish, combine the garlic, tomatoes, onion, pepper and thyme sprigs. Drizzle with olive oil, a dash of balsamic, sprinkle of sea salt and black pepper and a dash of sugar (to add some sweetness). Combine well.
- Place on the high rack and cook at 190°C for 20–30 minutes.
- Move the dish to the bottom of the halogen. Place the grilling rack over the top, ready to grill your fish (see the section on Grilling in Chapter 1 for tips). Turn the temperature up to 240°C.
- Rub the fish with a little olive oil and season to taste. Place on the grilling rack and cook for approximately 8 minutes, or until the fish is cooked to your taste. Note that the cooking time also depends on how close to the heat the coley is, as this can vary according to the machine and equipment used.
- Remove from the oven and place on the plates. Spoon over the sauce and serve with a green salad.

Note: You could add some capers to the sauce. If you like things a bit spicy, add a chopped chilli.

3 cloves garlic, roughly chopped
250g punnet cherry tomatoes
1 large red onion, finely chopped
1 red pepper, roughly chopped
2–3 sprigs of thyme (or 3–4 sprigs of rosemary, or a small handful of oregano or basil)
Olive oil
Balsamic vinegar
Sea salt
Black pepper
Sugar
4 coley fillets

Simple Baked Tuna in White Wine

SERVES 4

1 onion, cut into rings
4 tuna fillets
2 cloves garlic, crushed
4 teaspoons butter
Small handful of parsley, chopped
Seasoning to taste
4 tablespoons white wine

If you like to plan your meals ahead, this can be prepared in the morning and left wrapped in the parcels, in the fridge all day until you are ready to cook them. Simply place in the halogen, along with some mini roasties or pop some new potatoes and green vegetables to cook, and you have a perfect, stress-free meal.

• Prepare 4 squares of foil, big enough to parcel the fish. (You may also want to line this with parchment or you can buy from Lakeland parchment with a foil backing.)
• Place the onion rings on each foil square. Pop the tuna on top of the onion rings.
• Add ½ crushed clove of garlic to each parcel. Finish with 1 teaspoon of butter, a sprinkle of fresh parsley and season to taste.
• Fold the edges of the foil up until secure and almost ready to close. Then carefully add 1 tablespoon of wine to each parcel before sealing completely.
• Place the parcels on the low rack and cook at 190°C for 15–20 minutes or until the fish flakes easily.
• Serve with new potatoes and green vegetables.

Simple Garlic and Dill Salmon

SERVES 4

- Place the garlic, dill, lemon zest and olive oil in a food processor and combine well to form a runny paste. Season with black pepper.
- Place the fillets, skin-side down, in the bottom of a greased baking dish.
- Pour over the paste and cover with clingfilm. Leave to marinate for 1 hour in the fridge.
- When you are ready to cook, remove the clingfilm and place the dish on the high rack. Set the temperature to 200°C and cook for 15 minutes or until the salmon flakes easily.
- Serve with new potatoes and salad.

4 cloves garlic
Handful of fresh dill
Zest of 1 lemon
75ml olive oil
Black pepper
4 salmon fillets

Chilli and Spring Onion Mackerel

SERVES 4

4 tablespoons olive oil

3 cloves garlic, finely chopped

3 red chillies, finely chopped

5 spring onions, finely chopped

Juice and zest of 1 lemon

Seasoning

4 mackerel, cleaned, heads removed and gutted

A great summer dish, perfect for alfresco dining.

• Place the oil, garlic, chillies, spring onions and lemon juice and zest in a bowl and combine well. Season to taste.

• Using a sharp knife, score the top of the fish, in regular slits, exposing the flesh.

• Place the fish onto a baking tray. Carefully spoon some of the sauce mixture into the slits, rubbing into the skin where possible.

• Place the tray onto the grilling rack (see the section on Grilling in Chapter 1 for tips). Turn the temperature to 240°C and effectively grill the fish on each side until cooked, adding more sauce as you turn. Aim for approximately 8 minutes each side, though the cooking time can vary depending on the machine and equipment used, and the size of the fish.

• Remove from the oven and place the fish on plates ready to serve. Pour the remaining juice over the fish. Serve with crusty bread and a green salad.

Creamy Stuffed Monkfish

SERVES 4

You may be familiar with the stuffed chicken dishes where you make a pocket in the chicken fillet and fill it with cream cheese or similar, before wrapping in bacon. This is made in a similar way using monkfish fillets. You can use other fish fillets, but they need to be quite thick to allow you to make the pocket. In this recipe I have used a simple cream cheese and herb stuffing, and wrapped the fish in Parma ham, but why not experiment with your own versions.

150g cream cheese
Zest and juice of ½ lemon
2 cloves garlic, crushed
Small handful of fresh, mixed herbs (oregano, rosemary, basil, parsley and/or thyme)
Seasoning
4 monkfish fillets
12–14 rashers Parma ham
Olive oil

- In a bowl, mix the cream cheese, lemon zest and juice, garlic and herbs together. Season to taste.
- Using a very sharp knife, carefully make a slit in each fillet, big enough for you to stuff.
- Carefully stuff each fillet with the cream cheese mixture and wrap with the Parma ham to secure. Try to place the loose ends of the ham on the base of the fillet. If you are unsure, you can use a wooden cocktail stick (ideally having been soaked in water to avoid burning) to hold it in place.
- Place the finished fillets onto a greased baking tray. Season and drizzle with olive oil.
- Place on the high rack and cook at 190°C for 12–18 minutes, until the fish is cooked and the Parma ham is starting to brown.
- Serve with mini roast potatoes and green vegetables.

Easy Chilli, Garlic and Ginger Baked Prawns

SERVES 4

2–3 cloves of garlic

3cm knuckle of ginger, finely chopped

8 spring onions, finely chopped

1–2 chillies, finely chopped

1 stem of lemongrass, peeled and finely chopped

Zest and juice of 1 large lemon

2 tablespoons olive oil

1 tablespoon oyster sauce

2–3 tablespoons water

Seasoning

Handful of coriander leaves, finely chopped

150g green beans, trimmed and halved

1kg king or tiger prawns, peeled

A really simple meal. Prepare it in advance and keep in the fridge ready to parcel up when required.

- In a large bowl, mix the garlic, ginger, spring onions, chillies, lemongrass, lemon zest and juice, olive oil, oyster sauce and water together. Season to taste.
- Add the coriander, beans and prawns and toss until thoroughly mixed.
- Cut one large piece of foil (make sure this is big enough!) and line this with parchment. (You can buy foil backed with parchment from Lakeland.) Spray or brush with olive oil. Bring up the sides of the foil to form a bowl shape, leaving enough foil to bring in and seal when necessary. I find sitting the foil in a bowl helps keep the shape and avoids mess.
- Carefully pour or spoon the mixture into the foil parcel. Bring up the edges and secure well.
- Place on the low rack and cook at 200°C for 18–25 minutes, depending on the size of the prawns.
- Remove from the oven and leave to rest for 5 minutes before transferring into a large serving dish. You can serve this with crusty bread or a bed of fluffy rice.

Baked Trout with Almonds

SERVES 4

- Rub the cleaned trout with olive oil and season with black pepper.
- Place each fish on its own sheet of aluminium foil (you may also want to line this with parchment or you can buy from Lakeland parchment with a foil backing), big enough to parcel up.
- Spray each sheet with olive oil (or brush if you don't have spray). Place the fish in the centre of the foil and fold up the sides to form a bowl shape, secure enough to hold melted butter.
- In a saucepan on your hob, melt the butter over a medium heat. Then add the lemon juice, zest and almonds and warm for 1–2 minutes, stirring constantly.
- Remove from the heat and pour over each fish, ensuring they are evenly covered. Secure the foil parcels well.
- Place on the high rack, set the temperature to 190°C and cook for 20–30 minutes. The cooking time depends on the size of the fish – when cooked, the fish will flake easily when forked.
- Remove the fish from the parcels (be careful as it is very hot) and serve, pouring any excess juice back over the fish.
- Serve with green vegetables and new, minted potatoes.

4 small trout, cleaned and gutted
Olive oil
Black pepper
60g butter
Juice and zest of 1 large lemon
80g flaked almonds

4–6 spring onions,
   finely chopped
60g butter
150g mature Cheddar
2 teaspoons
   wholegrain mustard
3 tablespoons crème
   fraîche
Seasoning
4 cod fillets

Cheesy Grilled Cod

- In a bowl, mix the spring onions, butter, cheese, mustard and crème fraîche. Season to taste.
- Place the fish fillets on a baking tray. Turn the halogen to 250°C. Place the fish on the grilling rack (see the section on Grilling in Chapter 1 for tips).
- Grill on both sides for 4–5 minutes per side. (The cooking time may vary depending on the machine, thickness of the fillets and height of your rack.)
- Carefully place the cheese mixture onto the fillets and continue to cook until golden and bubbling. The fish should be flaking and the cheese golden.
- Serve with a lovely salad.

Creamy Ginger and Lemon Haddock Bake

- Wash the haddock fillets and place them in the bottom of an ovenproof dish.
- Mix the crème fraîche, milk, lemon zest, ginger, mustard and parsley together. Season to taste. Pour over the fish fillets until evenly covered.
- Sprinkle the top of the bake with paprika.
- Place on the high rack and set the temperature to 190°C. Bake for 20–25 minutes, or until the fish is cooked to your taste.
- Serve with wilted spinach.

4 haddock fillets
250g crème fraîche
100ml milk
Zest of 1 lemon
2–3cm knuckle of
  ginger, chopped
2 teaspoons
  wholegrain mustard
Small handful of
  chopped parsley
Seasoning
Paprika

Chilli and Ginger Crab au Gratin

Olive oil
1 onion, finely
  chopped
1 chilli, finely
  chopped
3cm knuckle of ginger,
  chopped
3 cloves garlic,
  crushed
400g crab meat
100g sweetcorn
3 teaspoons light soy
  sauce
Black pepper
Sea salt
100g breadcrumbs
30g Parmesan cheese

- Drizzle a little olive oil into a sauté pan on your hob. Add the onion, chilli, ginger and garlic, and cook over a medium heat for a minute or two to help soften.
- Add the crab meat and combine well. Cook for another couple of minutes.
- Finally add the sweetcorn and soy sauce. Season to taste.
- Place the mixture in 4 ramekin dishes, filling over-full. Press the mixture down.
- In a bowl, mix the breadcrumbs, Parmesan and seasoning together. Sprinkle this over the ramekin dishes.
- When you are ready to cook, place the ramekin dishes on the high rack. Turn the temperature to 210°C and cook for 10–15 minutes or until golden.
- Serve immediately with crisp green salad.

Salmon, Potato and Chive Fish Cakes

SERVES 4-6

- In a food processor, combine the potato (this is easier if warm), salmon, spring onions, chives and lemon zest. Add 2 of the beaten eggs and season to taste.
- Form into balls and flatten.
- Dip each cake into the remaining beaten egg, ensuring it is well covered. (If the cakes are sticky, you won't need to do this.) Then dip into the breadcrumbs, again ensuring it is well covered. Then place onto a greased or lined baking tray.
- When you are ready to cook, set the temperature to 250°C. Place the cakes on the grilling rack (see the section on Grilling in Chapter 1 for tips).
- Grill them on each side until cooked through – approximately 8–10 minutes each side depending on your machine and height of the rack.
- Serve immediately or they can be eaten cold.

500g cooked potato, mashed
350g salmon (tinned)
½ bunch of spring onions, finely chopped
Handful of chopped chives
Zest of 1 lemon
2 eggs, beaten
1 egg, beaten separately (optional)
Seasoning
100g breadcrumbs

Mackerel Bake

SERVES 4

1kg new potatoes
4 mackerel fillets,
    cooked and flaked
1 onion, sliced
600g crème fraîche
200ml milk
2 tablespoons
    wholegrain mustard
Black pepper
100g breadcrumbs
50g oats
50g mature cheese (I
    use Cheddar)

- Boil or steam the new potatoes until almost soft. Then drain and thickly slice.
- Grease your ovenproof dish (I use a deep Pyrex). Place a layer of potato on the base, followed by some flaked mackerel and onion. Repeat, finishing with a layer of potato.
- Combine the crème fraîche with the milk and mustard. Season to taste. Pour this over the layers.
- Combine the breadcrumbs, oats and cheese and sprinkle this on top of the dish. Season with black pepper.
- Place on the high rack. Set the temperature to 200°C and cook for 20–25 minutes until golden and bubbling.
- Serve with salad for a fabulous supper.

Baked Swordfish with Mango and Ginger Sauce

SERVES 4

- Prepare a square of foil, big enough to parcel the fish fillets. (You may also want to line this with parchment or you can buy from Lakeland parchment with a foil backing.)
- Place the onion rings on the foil square. Pop the swordfish on top of the onion rings.
- Mix the lemon juice, zest, ginger and mango chutney together to form a paste. Season with black pepper.
- Fold the edges of the foil up until secure and almost ready to close. Carefully add the paste to the parcel before sealing completely.
- Place the parcel on the low rack and cook at 200°C for 20 minutes or until the fish flakes easily.
- Serve with new potatoes and green vegetables.

1 onion, sliced
4 swordfish steaks
Juice and zest of 1 lemon
3cm knuckle of ginger, finely chopped
4 tablespoons mango chutney
Black pepper

Garlic and Herb-crusted Cod with Parsley Sauce

SERVES 4

4 cod fillets
2–3 cloves garlic
Generous handful of
  parsley
Some chives
Zest of 1 lemon
Juice of ½ lemon
75g breadcrumbs
50g butter
15g plain flour
300ml milk
Generous handful of
  parsley, chopped
Seasoning

- Place the fillets on a greased baking tray.
- In a food processor, combine the garlic, 1 handful of parsley, chives, lemon zest and juice, breadcrumbs and 25g butter. Once combined, season to taste.
- Place this mixture onto the top of the cod fillets, pushing down to ensure they are evenly and thickly coated.
- Place on the high rack and bake at 190°C for 15 minutes, or until the fish is flaking easily and cooked to your liking.
- While the fish is cooking, melt the remaining butter in a saucepan on your hob over a medium heat. Add the flour and stir with a wooden spoon to form a paste. Gradually add the milk and keep beating. If lumps form you can swap to a balloon whisk and beat out the lumps. Continue to cook until it starts to thicken. Add the second handful of parsley and season to taste. Leave until the fish is ready – you can reheat just as you are serving.
- When the fish is cooked, place on the plate with a generous dollop of parsley sauce alongside. Serve with new potatoes and green vegetables.

Vegetable and Halibut Pot Roast

- In a deep baking tray, drizzle a little olive oil. Place the fish, onion, red pepper, garlic and cherry tomatoes in the tray and combine until evenly distributed.
- Add the capers and thyme and drizzle again with olive oil. Finish with a sprinkle of balsamic vinegar and season with black pepper.
- Cover the tray with foil, making sure it is secure.
- Set the halogen to 200°C. Place on the high rack and cook for 20 minutes.
- Remove the foil and continue to cook for another 5 minutes.
- Serve with new potatoes.

Olive oil
4 halibut fillets
2 red onions, cut into wedges
2 red peppers, cut into thick slices or wedges
3–4 cloves garlic, roughly chopped
12–16 cherry tomatoes
2 tablespoons capers
3 sprigs of thyme
Balsamic vinegar
Black pepper

SERVES 4–6

1kg king prawns, de-
veined
8 tablespoons jalfrezi
curry sauce
100ml water
Handful of coriander,
chopped
1 lemon, cut into
wedges

Simple Jalfrezi Prawns

Nothing could be simpler!

- Place the prawns in an ovenproof dish.
- Mix the curry sauce and water together and pour this over the prawns. Leave to marinate in the fridge for 1 hour.
- Place a baking tray on the grilling rack (see the section on Grilling in Chapter 1 for tips).
- Carefully place the prawns on the tray. Turn the heat to high and grill, turning regularly until they go pink. This should take about 8 minutes, but cooking times can vary depending on the height of your rack and machine used.
- While they are grilling, heat the leftover sauce. Add the coriander.
- When the prawns are ready to serve, place them on a serving plate and pour over the remaining sauce. Garnish with more coriander. Serve with lemon wedges.

Fennel and Garlic Red Snapper

- In a sauté pan on your hob, heat some olive oil over a medium heat and add the onion, garlic and fennel. Cook until the fennel is soft. Then remove from the heat.
- Stir in the lemon zest, parsley and butter and season to taste. Stuff the red snapper with the mixture.
- Place the snapper in a baking tray. Pour over the vermouth and lemon juice. Season to taste, before covering with foil.
- Place on the high rack and cook for 20–25 minutes at 200°C. The fish should be easily flaked with a fork when it is cooked.
- Serve immediately with new potatoes and green vegetables.

Olive oil
1 white onion, finely chopped
5 cloves garlic, roughly chopped
½ bulb of fennel, finely chopped
Zest of 1 lemon
Handful of fresh parsley, chopped
30g butter
Seasoning
1 red snapper, cleaned and boned
100ml vermouth
Juice of 1 lemon

Spinach and Salmon Mornay

SERVES 4

2 tablespoons butter
2 tablespoons plain
   flour
350ml milk
110g Gruyère cheese,
   grated
1 tablespoon
   wholegrain mustard
Black pepper
60g baby leaf spinach
225g salmon, flaked
   (pre-cooked or
   tinned)
50g breadcrumbs
25g grated Parmesan

- In a saucepan, melt the butter on a medium heat. Using a wooden spoon, stir in the flour and keep stirring until it starts to form a paste.
- Gradually add the milk and continue to stir. If lumps start to form, switch to a balloon whisk and beat well.
- When the sauce starts to thicken, you can add the grated cheese, wholegrain mustard and black pepper to taste. Leave to one side and start to prepare the rest of the dish.
- Place the spinach in a colander and wash under hot water so it starts to wilt. Place in the bottom of a greased ovenproof dish (or individual ramekin dishes).
- Place the flaked fish into the dish and cover with the cheese sauce.
- Finish with a sprinkle of breadcrumbs and Parmesan. Season again with black pepper.
- Place on the high rack and set the temperature to 200°C. Cook for 15 minutes until golden and bubbling.
- Serve immediately.

Salmon and Watercress Frittata

SERVES 4

- Grease a deep dish. Place on the medium rack and set the temperature to 190°C.
- Meanwhile, combine the eggs and double cream in a large jug or bowl. Add the onion, salmon and watercress and season with black pepper, sea salt and freshly grated nutmeg.
- Open the lid of the halogen and carefully pour the mixture into the dish, ensuring it is evenly covered.
- Place the lid back down and cook for 20–25 minutes until golden and puffed.
- Serve with a lovely green salad.

6 eggs, beaten
100ml double cream
1 small onion, finely chopped
400g tin salmon, flaked
75g watercress, chopped
Black pepper
Sea salt
½ teaspoon nutmeg, freshly grated

Vegetarian

6

You don't have to be a vegetarian to enjoy vegetarian food. From a nutritional point of view, I would advise people to have at least two meat-free days a week. A diet rich in fresh, wholesome vegetables, fruit, nuts and seeds, along with oily fish, is really what we should all strive for. This chapter contains some simple dishes which should appeal to all tastes.

Cheese and eggs do appear frequently, simply because that is what many people love, but if you are watching your weight and cholesterol levels, try to cut down on the cheese consumption. There are many half-fat/low-fat Cheddars on the market now which work really well in most recipes, and tastewise they are really no different.

Spicy Roasted Sweet Potato with Yoghurt Dressing

SERVES 4

3 sweet potatoes, diced
  to the same size
2 red onions,
  quartered
2–4 cloves garlic,
  roughly chopped
Drizzle of olive oil
1 chilli
2.5–5cm knuckle of
  fresh ginger
2 teaspoons coriander
  seeds
2 teaspoons cumin
  seeds
1 teaspoon turmeric
Seasoning
Handful of fresh
  coriander leaves,
  chopped
2–3 tablespoons thick
  yoghurt (I prefer
  using Greek yoghurt
  such as Total)

• Place the sweet potatoes, onion and garlic into your ovenproof dish. Coat/toss well in the olive oil. Place on the low rack and cook for 10 minutes at 200°C.

• Meanwhile, chop the chilli, grate the ginger and crush the coriander, cumin and turmeric. Mix together thoroughly. Season to taste.

• Once the timer beeps to indicate the 10 minutes are up, lift the lid of the halogen and sprinkle the spices over the vegetables. Carefully toss again, ensuring it is all covered well. If necessary, you can add a little more oil but it should not be soaked in oil – just lightly covered.

• Turn the halogen back on at 200°C for another 15–20 minutes until the potatoes are soft.

• Then remove and place in a serving dish. Add the chopped coriander leaves and serve with a dollop of yoghurt.

Mediterranean-style Roasted Vegetables

This is a really easy dish, suitable to eat on its own with the crumbled feta or goat's cheese, or to use as a pasta sauce/base or even as a pizza topping.

- Prepare the vegetables and place into an ovenproof dish, ensuring they are evenly distributed.
- Mix the olive oil, balsamic, sugar, oregano and seasoning together. Pour this over the vegetables before tossing well ensuring the vegetables are evenly covered.
- Turn on the halogen to 200°C. Place the ovenproof dish on the low rack and cook for 20–30 minutes until the vegetables are soft.
- To serve, sprinkle with fresh Italian herbs and crumbled goat's cheese or feta.

SERVES 4

2 red onions, quartered
3–4 cloves garlic, roughly chopped
1 aubergine, thickly sliced
2 courgettes, thickly sliced
8–12 vine tomatoes
2 red peppers, quartered
Drizzle of olive oil
Dash of balsamic vinegar
1 teaspoon sugar
2 teaspoons dried oregano
Seasoning

SERVES 2–4

150g plain flour
2 eggs
150ml milk
125–150g mature
  Cheddar, grated
½ small onion, finely
  chopped
6–8 sundried
  tomatoes, drained
  and chopped
1–2 teaspoons dried
  oregano
Seasoning
2–3 tablespoons good
  quality, thick pasta
  sauce
1 tomato, thinly sliced

Eggy Pizza

This is a really yummy and very easy recipe. I saw Nigella making something similar and I wondered if it could be adapted to work in the halogen. Yes, it can and it's a really big favourite of my youngest son. You can of course choose whatever topping and filling ingredients you wish, but I find this works wonderfully.

• Place the flour in a bowl. Beat the eggs and milk together. Pour this onto the flour and mix well. Add two-thirds of the grated cheese, the onion, sundried tomatoes and half the oregano. Season to taste.
• Pour this into a greased baking dish or tray – I use a Victoria sponge tin but you can use a Pyrex dish or anything with sides. Make sure this fits in your halogen oven.
• Place on the high rack and cook for 20 minutes at 190°C.
• When the timer goes off, spread the top of the omelette/pizza with your pasta sauce. Finish with the remaining cheese and oregano, and the slices of tomato. You could add anything else: pepperoni, goat's cheese instead of Cheddar, peppers, mushrooms, etc.
• Bake again for another 10 minutes before serving with a salad. A great supper!

Courgette and Parmesan Frittata

A simple, classic frittata made in the halogen – perfect for a quick lunch or supper. For those who prefer to make this in the conventional way, you can follow the same steps using the hob and place it in the halogen for the final 3–4 minutes.

- Select a non-stick dish which has at least 2–3cm sides. I use a round cake tin. Make sure it fits well in your halogen.
- Place the butter and olive oil in the dish and add the onion and garlic.
- Place on the grilling rack (see the section on Grilling in Chapter 1 for tips) and cook at 230°C until it starts to soften. You may want to stir occasionally to prevent burning. This should only take approximately 5–8 minutes.
- Once soft, add the courgettes.
- Whilst they are cooking, beat the eggs with the seasoning and two-thirds of the Parmesan. Pour this over the courgettes and leave to cook until firm and golden – this should take no more than 10 minutes.
- 2–3 minutes before serving, add a final sprinkle of Parmesan and leave until it becomes golden.
- Serve immediately with a lovely fresh salad – the perfect quick supper.

SERVES 4

30g butter
Drizzle of olive oil
1 red onion, finely chopped
1–2 cloves garlic, roughly chopped
200g courgettes, finely sliced
6 eggs
Seasoning
40g Parmesan, grated

Vegetable and Tofu Burgers

SERVES 4–6

200g tofu, mashed
1 red onion, finely
  chopped
2–3 cloves garlic, finely
  chopped
½ red chilli, finely
  chopped
½ red pepper, finely
  chopped
1 large or 2 medium
  carrots, grated
1 courgette, grated
75g wholemeal
  breadcrumbs
1 egg, beaten
Seasoning

Don't think these are only suitable for sandal-wearing vegetarians. They are absolutely delicious and a great alternative to the heavy fattiness of meat. Give them a go with grilled, chilli halloumi and serve with fresh bread rolls or bagels.

- In a bowl, mash the tofu. Add the remaining ingredients and combine well before seasoning to taste.
- Form into burgers and place on a greased baking tray. If you don't want to cook immediately, you can refrigerate them wrapped in parchment, or freeze, leaving parchment between each burger to prevent them from freezing stuck together.
- When ready to cook, place on the grilling rack (see the section on Grilling in Chapter 1 for tips) on the highest heat and grill for 5–8 minutes on each side until golden.
- Serve immediately.

Cheese and Herb Soufflés

SERVES 4–6

I know you are probably thinking that soufflés are not quick and easy, but really, they are. We all fear soufflés, but with practice they can be straightforward. Give them a try and you know what they say, practice makes perfect.

- Begin by making a roux, which is a basic start to a white sauce. Melt the butter in a pan and add the flour, stirring well with a wooden spoon to avoid lumps. Add the milk and change to a balloon whisk (this helps avoid lumps). Cook until it thickens and then remove from the heat.
- Add the ricotta and Parmesan, followed by the egg yolks, herbs and seasoning. Combine well.
- Put the egg whites in a clean bowl (this should not have any grease on it or the egg whites won't fluff up). Beat until they form stiff peaks. Then fold in a spoonful of the ricotta mixture as this will help loosen the egg whites and help you combine the rest of the mixture.
- Once you have done this you can then add the egg whites to the rest of the cheese mixture and fold carefully. Don't over fold or they could go flat.
- Grease your soufflé dishes and pour in the mixture until it reaches the top.
- Place the soufflés in a deep tray, first making sure it fits in your halogen. Fill the tray with hot water until it reaches halfway up the soufflé dishes.
- Place on the high rack and set the temperature to 180°C. Cook for 20–25 minutes until firm, risen and golden but with a soft centre.
- Serve immediately before they slump.

50g butter
40g plain flour
150ml milk
250g ricotta cheese
25g Parmesan cheese, grated
4 eggs, separated
2 egg whites
Handful of fresh herbs, chopped (such as parsley, thyme, chives, oregano or rosemary)
Seasoning

Roasted Vegetable Ratatouille

SERVES 4

2 red peppers, cut into thick wedges

2 red onions, cut into wedges

4–5 cloves garlic, halved

8–10 tomatoes, scored but left whole

1 small aubergine, cut into thick wedges

2 courgettes, cut into lengthways wedges

Olive oil

Balsamic vinegar

Sea salt

Sugar

Fresh thyme and rosemary sprigs

1 jar passata

Black pepper

Simply yet totally delicious! Just chop and go!

- In your ovenproof dish, combine all the vegetables. Pour over a drizzle of olive oil, a dash of balsamic and a sprinkle of sea salt and sugar. Add the herb sprigs and toss again to ensure it is all evenly coated.
- Place on the high rack and cook at 200°C for 20 minutes.
- Add the passata and combine well. Season with black pepper.
- Place back in the oven and cook for another 10 minutes.
- Serve with crusty bread. For added yumminess, add some cubed feta cheese before serving.

Courgette, Parmesan and Chilli Patties

SERVES 4

These are gorgeous – perfect for a lovely supper on a summer's evening. I serve them with a selection of dips, new potato salad and green salads, or for quick snacks, some sweet chilli dip.

Olive oil
2–3 cloves garlic, crushed
Small bunch of spring onions, finely sliced
1–2 chillies, finely sliced (depending on taste)
4–5 courgettes, grated
3 eggs
75g crème fraîche
40g Parmesan cheese, grated
Seasoning

- On your hob, heat a little olive oil in a sauté pan over a medium heat. Add the garlic, spring onion and chilli and cook for 2–3 minutes. Then add the courgettes. Cook until soft, then remove from the heat.
- In a bowl, mix the eggs, crème fraîche and Parmesan together. Season to taste before adding the vegetables.
- Combine well. Form into patties and place on a well greased baking tray.
- Place the tray on the high rack and set the halogen to 220°C. Cook for 10–15 minutes until golden.
- Serve with salad or on their own with sweet chilli sauce.

Slow Cook Tuscan-style Tomato and Beans

SERVES 4

1–2 red onions, cut into thick slices

8–10 tomatoes, cut into thick wedges

1–2 red peppers, cut into thick wedges

4 cloves garlic, roughly chopped

Olive oil

Balsamic vinegar

Sea salt

Black pepper

Sugar

2–3 sprigs of thyme

1 x 400g tin cannelloni beans

1 x 400g tin mixed beans

150ml red wine

I love this dish. I tend to make a large batch and it lasts me a few meals – a lovely lunch with crusty bread, add pasta and you have a more filling meal, or simply serve it on its own with a handful of crumbled feta. Delicious!

- Into an ovenproof dish, put the onions, tomatoes, peppers and garlic. Prepare the vegetables so that they are chunky but small enough to eat.
- Drizzle over some olive oil and a dash of balsamic vinegar. Finish with a sprinkle of sea salt, black pepper and a little sugar to help sweeten.
- Add the thyme sprigs and combine well, ensuring everything is well distributed and coated in the oil.
- Place on the high rack and turn the temperature to 200°C. Cook for 20 minutes until it starts to soften. You will be surprised how much liquid comes out of this.
- Remove from the oven. Stir in the drained beans and add the wine. Place back in the oven for another 10 minutes until thoroughly cooked and the beans are warmed through.

Cauliflower and Broccoli Cheese Gratin

SERVES 4

- Cut your cauliflower and broccoli into equally sized florets. Steam or boil until they are only just soft. They should still have a bite and a little hardness to them – you certainly don't want a soggy mash!
- Meanwhile, place the butter in a saucepan and melt gently on a medium heat (not high!). Add the flour or cornflour and stir well with a wooden spoon. Add a little milk at a time, continuing to stir to avoid lumps.
- Switch now to a balloon whisk. Continue to stir over a medium heat until the sauce begins to thicken. The balloon whisk will also help eradicate any lumps that may have materialised. Add more milk as necessary to get the desired thickness – it should be the consistency of custard.
- Add the 100g mature Cheddar and mustard and season with black pepper. Keep stirring until the cheese has melted. Taste to see if you need more cheese or seasoning.
- Place the cooked cauliflower and broccoli in your ovenproof dish. Pour over the cheese sauce.
- In a bowl, mix together the breadcrumbs, oats, carrots and Cheddar or Parmesan. Season to taste. Pour over the cauliflower and broccoli cheese mixture.
- Place on the high rack and cook at 200°C for 20 minutes until golden.

1 small head of cauliflower
1 small head of broccoli
30g butter
20g plain flour or cornflour
400ml milk
100g mature Cheddar, grated
½ teaspoon mustard
Seasoning
120g wholemeal breadcrumbs
50g oats
2 medium carrots, grated
30g Cheddar or Parmesan, grated

Baked Ricotta Loaf with Slow-cooked Tomato and Basil Salad

SERVES 4–6

750g ricotta
100g fresh Parmesan, finely grated (not prepackaged grated as it does not have the same flavour)
2 eggs, beaten
Seasoning
400g vine tomatoes (ideally still on the vine)
1 red onion, cut into wedges
4–6 cloves garlic, finely chopped
Basil leaves
Olive oil
Balsamic vinegar

This is a really easy dish. The baked ricotta is easy to make and can be made a day in advance. Simply slice and serve with your chosen salad or accompaniment. I have chosen slow-cooked tomatoes and basil, as I love the flavours.

• In a bowl, mix the ricotta with the Parmesan. Fold in the beaten eggs. Season to taste.
• Line a large loaf tin with lining paper and grease well. Pour the ricotta mixture into the tin. Smooth the surface and press down gently. I normally give the tin a couple of firm taps on the worktop to displace any air pockets or bubbles.
• Place on the high rack and set the temperature to 210°C. Cook for 25–30 minutes until golden and firm. Then leave to cool.
• When you are ready to cook (immediately or a day later), place the tomatoes, onion, garlic and a few basil leaves in an ovenproof dish. Drizzle with olive oil and a dash of balsamic vinegar. Season with sea salt and black pepper.
• Place on the high rack and cook at 220°C for 15–20 minutes until the tomatoes are starting to wrinkle and turn a little brown.
• When ready to serve, slice the ricotta loaf into thick slices. Place one slice on each plate. Add a generous spoonful of the slow-cooked vine tomatoes to the side of the ricotta slice. Drizzle with some extra virgin olive oil, add a few more basil leaves and season with black pepper.

Warm Beetroot Salad

SERVES 4

- Place the root vegetables (all cubed to a similar size) in a tin or browning tray.
- Drizzle with olive oil, ensuring it is all evenly coated. Sprinkle with oregano, sea salt, black pepper and a drizzle of balsamic.
- Place on the high rack and set to 210°C. Cook for 20 minutes, or until soft and sweet.
- Meanwhile, place the leaf salad in your serving dishes. Add the chopped red onion (or spring onions) and the red pepper. Toss to ensure it is evenly distributed.
- When the vegetables are cooked, simply place them in the centre of your leaf salad, finishing with a sprinkle of feta or goat's cheese. Serve immediately.

2–3 beetroots, peeled and cubed
2–3 parsnips, peeled and cubed
1–2 small sweet potato, peeled and cubed
Olive oil
1 teaspoon dried oregano
Sea salt
Black pepper
Balsamic vinegar
4 generous handfuls of seasonal salad leaves, washed
1 red onion, sliced (or ½ bunch of spring onions, sliced)
1 red pepper, sliced
100g feta or soft goat's cheese

Roasted Vegetable Curry

SERVES 4

2 red onions, cut into wedges

1–2 sweet potatoes, thickly diced

1 potato, thickly diced

½ or 1 small butternut squash, unpeeled and cut into 2cm thick chunks or wedges

1–2 carrots, thickly sliced

Olive oil

Paprika

1 teaspoon coriander seeds

1 teaspoon cumin seeds

1 red chilli

4 cloves garlic

2.5cm knuckle of ginger

2 teaspoons turmeric

2–3 teaspoons garam masala

Small handful of coriander leaves

3–4 spring onions

Seasoning

300ml water

I adore curries and roasted vegetables so why not put the two together. It creates a very simple curry dish which tastes fantastic.

- Prepare the vegetables. Place the red onions, potatoes, butternut squash and carrots in an ovenproof dish (making sure it fits in your halogen). Drizzle with olive oil and a sprinkle of paprika and toss until combined, ensuring the vegetables are evenly coated in oil.
- Place the vegetables on the high rack and cook at 220°C for 20 minutes.
- Meanwhile, place the coriander seeds and cumin seeds in a large, dry sauté pan and heat gently on your hob for 1–2 minutes. When the fragrance starts to break through, place in a pestle and mortar and combine. Leave the sauté pan to one side as you will need this in a moment.
- Into your liquidiser, put the ground spices, chilli, garlic, ginger, turmeric, garam masala, coriander leaves, spring onions and seasoning. Combine well. Add olive oil until a more liquid paste is formed.
- Place this paste into the sauté pan and heat gently. Add the water and combine whilst bringing up to the boil. Once boiling turn off heat.
- Finally, add the coconut milk and Greek yoghurt to the curry paste in the sauté pan and combine well. Leave to one side.
- By now your vegetables should be almost ready for the next stage. Once the 15-minute timer beeps, add

the peppers and tomatoes and return for another 15 minutes. Combine well and add a drizzle more oil if necessary.

- Remove the vegetables from the halogen. Take the flesh of the butternut squash off the skin. Add these to your paste in the sauté pan. Add a little water if you want a more liquid curry, bearing in mind that some will evaporate during the cooking. Cook for another 5–10 minutes until the vegetables are cooked to your taste.
- Sprinkle with coriander leaves. Serve with fluffy, fragrant rice, yoghurt and chutney.

150–200ml low fat coconut milk

3 tablespoons Greek yoghurt

1 red pepper, thickly sliced

1 yellow pepper, thickly sliced

3–4 tomatoes, cut into wedges

Extra coriander leaves to sprinkle

150g plain flour (I use
  seeded bread flour
  as I like the nutty
  texture)
75g cold butter
Water
400–500g new
  potatoes, quartered
2 onions, chopped
100–150g mature
  Cheddar, grated
300ml full fat milk
2 eggs, beaten
3–6 cloves garlic,
  crushed (depending
  on your own taste)
Small handful of fresh
  parsley, finely
  chopped
Black pepper

New Potato Homity Pie

I am a sucker for freshly dug new potatoes, cooked with some garden mint and tossed in English butter. With this in mind, I thought I would share my Homity Pie recipe. Traditionally English, it is perfect for alfresco dining, lunchboxes or a cosy supper. It is also a fabulous way of using up any leftover new potatoes.

• Prepare your pastry first to allow some time for it to chill. If you will be preparing the pie in a hurry, you could consider making the pastry the night before and leaving it in the fridge in a freezer bag.
• I use a food processor, adding the flour and butter, pulsing until the flour resembles breadcrumbs, then adding a little water at a time until it forms a dough. If you are doing this in a bowl, rub the butter into the flour until it resembles breadcrumbs. Then using a knife, stir in a little ice cold water at a time, again until this forms a dough.
• Place the dough in a freezer bag and leave in the fridge for at least 20 minutes.
• When the pastry is ready, roll out and line a greased pastry dish – I use a 25cm flan dish. Prick with a fork before lining with baking parchment and filling with baking beans. (You can use dried chickpeas or dried rice if you don't have baking beans.) Place on the high rack and cook at 180°C for 10 minutes. Remove the beans and parchment and cook for another 5 minutes before removing from the oven.
• Meanwhile, steam your potatoes until they are just cooked – you don't want them soggy!

- Place the cooked potato evenly in your pastry dish. Add the chopped onion and half the cheese, again, making sure it is evenly spread.
- In a jug, put the milk, egg, garlic and parsley and season with black pepper (you should not need salt as the cheese will contain adequate salt). Combine well before pouring over the potato. Finish with the remaining cheese.
- Place back into the oven on the high rack and cook for another 20 minutes at 180°C until golden.
- Serve hot or cold with a lovely seasonal salad.

Healthy Bean and Sausage Bake

SERVES 4

4–8 vegetarian
    sausages
Olive oil
1 red onion, finely
    chopped
2 cloves garlic,
    crushed
1 red pepper, chopped
1 courgette, sliced
2 sticks of celery
1 tin tomatoes,
    chopped
1 tin baked beans
Black pepper
Sea salt
A few fresh basil leaves
    (or a sprinkle of
    dried oregano)

Kids love baked beans and sausages, but this recipe takes it a little further with some healthy vegetables thrown in. I have used veggie sausages in this recipe but you could use any meat sausage if you prefer.

- Place the sausages in a deep ovenproof dish and drizzle with a little olive oil.
- Place on the high rack and cook at 190°C for 10 minutes.
- Meanwhile, in a sauté pan on your hob, heat a little olive oil over a medium/high heat and add the onion, garlic and pepper. Cook until it starts to soften.
- Add the courgette and celery and cook for another few minutes.
- Add the tomatoes and baked beans. Before you throw the tins away, rinse them with a small amount of water and add this to the sauce (just a couple of centimetres for each tin). Season to taste and add a few leaves of fresh basil (or a sprinkle of dried oregano if your children don't like basil)
- Remove the sausages from the oven. Pour over the sauce and place back in the oven. Cook for another 15 minutes.
- Serve with cheesy mash for a really comforting supper.

Cheesy Stuffed Sweet Peppers

- Place the halved peppers on a baking tray. Drizzle with a little olive oil and sprinkle with sea salt, sugar and the garlic.
- In each half, add 4 halved cherry tomatoes. On top of this, add a few slices of red onion. Drizzle with a little more olive oil and place on the high rack.
- Turn the temperature to 190°C and cook for 15 minutes.
- Remove from the oven and add the basil leaves and mozzarella slices to the centre of the peppers.
- Place back in the oven and cook for another 10–15 minutes until golden.
- Serve immediately.

2–4 sweet peppers, halved lengthways
Olive oil
Sea salt
Sugar
2–3 cloves garlic, crushed
8–16 cherry tomatoes, halved
1 red onion, sliced
Handful of basil leaves
250g mozzarella, sliced
Seasoning

SERVES 4

2 x 400g tins
  chickpeas, drained
  and washed
3–4 cloves garlic,
  crushed
1 small onion
2 tablespoons tahini
  paste
1 egg
1–2 teaspoons ground
  cumin
1 teaspoon ground
  coriander
½ teaspoon chilli
  powder
Squeeze of lemon
  juice
3–4 tablespoons
  breadcrumbs

Falafels

I love these – they are so easy to make and delicious with a lovely selection of salads. Perfect alfresco food.

- Place all the ingredients, apart from the breadcrumbs, in a food processor and whizz until you have a moist paste.
- Scrape into a bowl and cover with clingfilm. Leave in the fridge for at least 2 hours to allow the flavours to develop.
- When you are ready, place the breadcrumbs into a plate or bowl. Scoop out a little of the mixture and form into balls – you may need to have floured hands for this as it does become sticky.
- Dip each ball into the breadcrumbs, ensuring it is roughly coated. Place the finished balls onto a greased non-stick baking tray.
- Pop the tray onto the high rack and cook at 200°C for 15–20 minutes, turning occasionally to ensure they are cooked and browned all over.
- Serve hot or cold with salads, or stuffed in pitta.

Cheese, Potato and Onion Squares

Ideal for using up any cooked potato. Delicious hot or cold.

- Combine all the ingredients together in a bowl. Don't worry if the potato becomes a bit like mash, it will still taste delicious.
- Place the mixture into a lined and greased ovenproof dish (I use a Pyrex dish). Finish with a sprinkle more cheese.
- Place on the high rack. Set the temperature to 200°c and cook for 20 minutes until golden.
- Cut into squares and serve hot or cold.

SERVES 4

400g cooked potato, diced
1 onion, finely chopped
Small handful of fresh chives, chopped
125–150g mature cheese, grated (I use Cheddar)
2 eggs, beaten
Black pepper
Sea salt (optional)
Extra grated cheese to sprinkle

SERVES 4

1 large red onion, cut
   into wedges
2 red peppers, cut into
   thick slices
3–4 cloves garlic,
   roughly chopped
2 courgettes, thickly
   sliced
1 aubergine, thickly
   sliced
2 sweet potatoes,
   thickly sliced
12 cherry tomatoes
Olive oil
Balsamic vinegar
Sea salt
Black pepper
Paprika
3 sprigs of rosemary
300g tagliatelle
Parmesan

Roasted Vegetable Tagliatelle

- Place the vegetables in a large bowl. Drizzle with olive oil, a dash of balsamic vinegar and sprinkle with sea salt, black pepper and paprika. Combine well, ensuring everything is evenly covered. Add more olive oil if needed.
- Pour the vegetables into your baking tray or ovenproof dish. Place the sprigs of rosemary in between the vegetables.
- Place the dish on the high rack and set the temperature to 200°C. Cook for 30 minutes.
- Five minutes before the vegetables are ready, bring a saucepan of water to the boil. Add the tagliatelle and cook as per the manufacturer's instructions. Then drain and mix in the vegetables.
- Serve with fresh Parmesan shavings.

Roasted Beetroot and Red Pepper Salad

SERVES 4

- Place the beetroot and red peppers on a baking tray. Drizzle with olive oil, ensuring they are evenly coated. Add some sprigs of rosemary.
- Place on the high rack and set to 180°C. Cook for 30–40 minutes until soft.
- Meanwhile, in a large serving dish, place the rocket and onion. Combine well.
- In a bowl or cup, mix 2–3 tablespoons of olive oil, the vinegar, sea salt and black pepper. Combine, adjusting vinegar and olive oil to taste.
- When the beetroot and peppers are roasted, you can either leave them to cool or immediately place on top of the rocket. Pour over the dressing and toss until combined.

Note: For extra flavour, why not add some diced feta cheese.

500g baby beetroot, halved
2–3 red peppers, quartered
Olive oil
Sprigs of rosemary
100g rocket
1 large red onion, diced
2 tablespoons red wine vinegar
Sea salt
Black pepper

SERVES 2

250g asparagus
Olive oil
Black pepper
2 eggs
80g salad leaves
Parmesan
Salad dressing

Grilled Asparagus and Poached Egg Salad

- Place the asparagus on a baking tray. Place the tray on the grilling rack (see the section on Grilling in Chapter 1 for tips). Drizzle with olive oil and season with black pepper.
- Set the temperature to 250°C and cook the asparagus for 8–10 minutes, until cooked to your taste.
- Meanwhile, boil the water for poaching the eggs and place the salad in your dishes.
- Approximately 3–4 minutes before the asparagus is ready, begin to poach the eggs.
- Remove the asparagus from the oven, and arrange over the salad leaves.
- Top with the poached eggs and finish with some Parmesan shavings, black pepper and a drizzle of salad dressing.

Spinach and Ricotta Pancake Bake

This is a really lovely meal – you can use readymade pancakes or make your own (the recipe for which follows this one).

- Place the spinach in a colander and run under hot water until it starts to wilt. Then put the spinach in a bowl.
- Add the chopped onion and ricotta and combine well. Mix in the Cheddar and season with black pepper and a grating of fresh nutmeg.
- Lay out your pancakes one at a time. Pop a line of the mixture across one side of each pancake and roll into a sausage. Then place each one in a greased ovenproof dish.
- Pour over the sauce and finish with the grated Parmesan.
- Place in the halogen oven on the high rack. Set the temperature to 200°C and cook for 25 minutes.
- Serve with a lovely green salad.

100g baby leaf spinach
1 onion, finely chopped
1 tub ricotta
50g mature Cheddar, grated
Black pepper
Nutmeg
6–8 pancakes (depending on size of ovenproof dish)
1 jar tomato pasta sauce
30g Parmesan cheese, grated

110g plain flour
2 eggs
250g milk

Pancakes (Basic Recipe)

Use this recipe to make your own pancakes. They can be frozen, but remember to place baking parchment between each layer beforehand. Simply place in the halogen on the high rack at 210°C for 5 minutes each side to heat through before serving.

- Place the flour, eggs and milk in a jug or bowl and whisk well.
- Leave in the fridge for at least 15 minutes, then whisk again.
- On your hob, heat some oil in a frying pan until it is very hot.
- Fill a ladle with the mixture and pour this into the frying pan. Tilt the pan until the base is completely covered with the mixture.
- After a minute or two the mixture should start to bubble slightly, the edges will start to cook and the bottom will start to brown. Carefully loosen the edges and flip over. Continue to cook for another few minutes – you can flip again if you want to check both sides.
- Serve immediately or place on a plate with baking parchment between each layer to prevent them from sticking.

Blue Cheese and Broccoli Frittata

SERVES 4

- Place the broccoli florets in boiling water and cook for 5–8 minutes.
- Grease a deep dish. Place on the high rack and set the temperature to 190°C.
- Meanwhile, combine the eggs and double cream in a large jug or bowl. Add the onion, broccoli, blue cheese, chives and season with black pepper and sea salt.
- Open the halogen's lid and carefully pour the mixture into the dish, ensuring it is evenly covered.
- Close the lid and cook for 20–25 minutes until golden and puffed.
- Serve with a lovely green salad.

1 head of broccoli, cut into florets
6 eggs, beaten
100ml double cream
1 small onion, finely chopped
175g blue cheese, crumbled
1–2 teaspoons chives, finely chopped
Black pepper
Sea salt

Warm Vegetable Salad with Puy Lentils and Goat's Cheese

SERVES 4

2 red onions, cut into wedges
2 peppers, red and yellow, cut into thick slices
2 sweet potatoes, unpeeled and cut into thick slices
1 courgette, sliced
10 cherry tomatoes
Olive oil
Sea salt
Black pepper
100g Puy lentils
2–3 sprigs of rosemary
100g goat's cheese, crumbled

- Chop the vegetables and place in an ovenproof dish. Drizzle with olive oil and sprinkle with sea salt and black pepper.
- Place on the high rack and cook at 200°C for 20 minutes, until soft and roasted.
- Meanwhile, place the Puy lentils in a saucepan. Cover with water and add the rosemary. Bring to the boil and simmer for 15–20 minutes. Drain, remove the rosemary and place in a large serving dish, or 4 individual dishes.
- Remove the vegetables from the oven and tip onto the Puy lentils. Add the crumbled goat's cheese. Serve immediately.

Cauliflower Cheese Bake

SERVES 4

- Chop the cauliflower into manageable florets.
- Place in a steamer and cook until the cauliflower is tender but not soft.
- Meanwhile, make the sauce. Melt the butter gently in a saucepan on a medium heat (not high!). Add the flour or cornflour and stir well with a wooden spoon. Add the milk a little at a time, continuing to stir to avoid lumps.
- Switch now to a balloon whisk. Continue to stir over a medium heat until the sauce begins to thicken. The balloon whisk will also help to eradicate any lumps that may have formed. Add more milk as necessary to get to the desired thickness. The sauce should be the thickness of custard.
- If you are using nutritional yeast flakes, add these before the grated cheese as they will reduce the amount of cheese you will need – taste as you go!. Add the cheese and mustard and stir well. Season with black pepper.
- When the cauliflower is ready, transfer to an ovenproof dish. Pour over the sauce ensuring all the cauliflower is covered.
- Mix the oats, breadcrumbs and Parmesan together thoroughly. Scatter this over the cheese sauce.
- Preheat the halogen oven using the preheat setting or set the temperature to 210°C.
- Place the bake on the low rack. Cook for 15–20 minutes until the top is golden and crispy.

1 large cauliflower
200g butter
20g plain flour or cornflour
450ml milk
2 tablespoons nutritional yeast flakes (optional)
120g mature cheese, grated
½ teaspoon mustard (optional)
3 tablespoons home-prepared wholemeal breadcrumbs
2 tablespoons oats
20g Parmesan cheese
Black pepper to taste

One Pot – Slow and Satisfying

7

People often ask me if it is possible to cook a casserole in a halogen. Of course! Below are some examples of how this works. If you are cooking for more than 60 minutes and have an oven with the dial timer instead of the digital, you will have to remember to turn the oven back on. These recipes could also be cooked on the hob without transferring, or if you have a slow cooker, they could easily go in it.

Remember that, when cooking casseroles, the cheaper the cuts of meat, the longer you may want to cook them to gain lovely tender meat chunks. You can still achieve this with the halogen simply by covering the dish with a lid or double sheet of tin foil and cooking on a lower heat for a longer period of time. As with most cooking, you will find your own way to what suits your taste.

Whole Chicken Casserole

This is a very simple dish and perfect for that satisfying dinner. If you have a digital halogen, you can preset the timer to suit, but if your oven (such as the JML oven) has a manual timer you will only be able to cook for 1 hour at a time and then reset the timer as required.

SERVES 6

1 whole chicken, prepared and ready to cook
1 lemon, halved
Olive oil
250g shallots
3–4 cloves garlic, roughly chopped
4 carrots, thickly diced
4 sticks of celery, thickly sliced
2 sweet potatoes, thickly diced
2 potatoes, thickly diced
2 leeks, thickly sliced
4 tomatoes, diced
2–3 sprigs of thyme
1–2 teaspoons paprika
Seasoning
500ml chicken stock (more may be necessary)
500ml white wine or vermouth

- Prepare your chicken for cooking (make sure it fits easily in your halogen!). Place the 2 lemon halves into the cavity of the chicken. Rub the skin with olive oil.
- Place your chicken breast-side down into the halogen oven, directly onto the base of the bowl.
- Place your vegetables around the chicken, ensuring they are evenly distributed. Finish with the thyme and sprinkle with the paprika. Season to taste.
- Heat the stock gently. Add the wine or vermouth and pour this around the chicken.
- Cook for 30 minutes at 180°C.
- Remove the chicken gently. Stir the vegetables, adding more chicken stock if necessary. Place the chicken back in the oven breast-side up. You may need to wiggle the chicken around in the bowl to make sure the vegetables don't get trapped underneath. Sprinkle the breast with a little more paprika and thyme and season.
- Cook at the same temperature for another 45–60 minutes until the chicken is cooked to taste. (Cooking time depends on the chicken's size and personal taste.)
- To serve, carve the chicken and spoon over the vegetable and stock mixture. Enjoy!

Beef and Vegetable Cobbler

SERVES 4

- Place the beef steak in a bowl and coat with the flour and paprika.
- Place some olive oil in an ovenproof casserole dish and heat on your hob over a medium heat. (Remember to make sure that your dish will fit comfortably into your halogen oven as you will need to transfer it later in the recipe.) Add the onion, leek, carrot and celery and cook for 2 minutes.
- Add the beef and cook for a further 3–4 minutes, stirring well to avoid it sticking.
- Gradually add the wine, beef stock, redcurrant jelly and mushrooms. Add the dried herbs or if you are using fresh herbs, add half now. Simmer for 10 minutes.
- Remove from the hob and place on the low rack of the halogen oven. Cover with a lid or double layer of foil, making sure it is secure. Cook for 40 minutes at 200°C.
- Meanwhile, place the flour in a bowl. Add the yoghurt, oil and parsley. Mix to form a soft dough. Place on a floured board and shape into individual balls. Flatten slightly.
- At this point, remove the casserole's lid or foil. Stir the casserole and add the remaining fresh herbs if you are using them. Add more beef stock if needed. Place the scones on the top of the casserole, forming a circle or completely covering the top.
- Continue to bake for another 20 minutes or until the scones are golden and fluffy. Serve immediately.

450g stewing beef
   steak, cut into cubes
50g plain flour
3 teaspoons paprika
Olive oil
1 onion, thickly diced
2 leeks, sliced
1 large carrot, diced
3 sticks of celery, diced
2 tablespoons
   redcurrant jelly
300ml red wine
400ml beef stock
   (more may be
   necessary)
125g button
   mushrooms
Handful of fresh herbs
   or 1 teaspoon mixed
   dried herbs

Cobbler/scone mix
100g self-raising flour
75ml natural yoghurt
2 tablespoons olive oil
Small handful parsley,
   chopped (or 1
   teaspoon dried
   parsley)

Chicken and Mushroom Casserole

SERVES 4

Drizzle or spray of olive oil

1–2 cloves garlic, roughly chopped

2 leeks, finely chopped

6 spring onions, finely chopped

300g chicken pieces

175g mushrooms

300ml white wine

500ml chicken stock

1 teaspoon cornflour

1 teaspoon paprika

100g French beans

1 teaspoon dried tarragon (or a handful of fresh tarragon)

• Heat a little olive oil in a sauté pan on your hob over a medium heat and cook the garlic, leek and spring onion for 2–3 minutes. Add the chicken and the mushrooms and cook for a further 5 minutes.

• Place the chicken mixture in a casserole dish (making sure it fits in your halogen oven). Add the wine and stock to the dish.

• Mix the cornflour with 10ml of water in a cup to form a smooth paste and add to the chicken pot.

• Add all the remaining ingredients.

• Place on the low rack and cook at 190°C for 35–40 minutes. If the casserole starts to form a skin on the top you can pop on the casserole lid, or securely wrap a piece of tin foil over the top of the dish.

• Serve with new potatoes and green beans.

Note: If you prefer a creamier sauce, add some Total Greek yoghurt or crème fraîche 5 minutes before serving.

Lamb and Apricot Casserole

- Heat the oil in a sauté or frying pan on your hob over a medium heat and cook the onion, garlic and lamb for 2–3 minutes.
- Add the harissa or hot chilli paste and stir well for 2 minutes.
- Place the lamb mixture in a casserole dish (making sure it fits comfortably in your halogen). Add all the remaining ingredients and combine well. Pop on the casserole lid or cover securely with tin foil.
- Place on the low rack and cook at 200°C for 50 minutes.
- Remove the lid and cook for another 10 minutes. Serve garnished with coriander leaves and a side dish of sour cream.

Drizzle or spray of olive oil
1 onion, chopped
2–3 cloves garlic, crushed
400g lamb, diced
3 teaspoons harissa paste or hot chilli paste
2 teaspoons ground cinnamon
300ml red wine
1 tin chopped tomatoes
400ml hot water or stock
1 tin chickpeas, drained
75g dried apricots, chopped
Fresh coriander leaves to garnish
Sour cream to serve

Beef, Vegetable and Horseradish Casserole

500g stewing beef
25g flour
3 teaspoons paprika
Seasoning
Olive oil
1 onion, diced
½ medium swede,
  cubed
2–3 carrots, sliced
2 potatoes, diced
1 parsnip, diced
30g pearl barley
2 level tablespoons
  horseradish sauce
750ml hot beef stock
  (a little more may be
  necessary)
Handful of fresh
  thyme
Handful of fresh
  parsley

- Chop the beef into cubes. Mix the flour and paprika together and season. Dip the beef into the flour, ensuring it is evenly coated.
- Select your ovenproof/hob-proof casserole dish, making sure it fits in your halogen oven. Place this on the hob and heat a little oil over a medium heat. (If your casserole dish is not hob-proof, use a sauté pan and transfer into the casserole dish before placing in the halogen oven.)
- Add the beef and onion and cook until the onion starts to soften and the beef browns.
- Add the vegetables and allow to sweat for 5 minutes before adding all remaining ingredients. Stir to ensure everything is evenly distributed. Continue to cook for 15 minutes.
- Cover the casserole dish with a lid or double layer of tin foil and then transfer to the low rack. Set the halogen to 170°C.
- Cook for 1 hour. Take a look to see how things are getting on, stirring to distribute the ingredients. At this point you may want to add more stock. Continue to cook for another 20–30 minutes or until cooked to your satisfaction.
- Serve immediately with dollops of fluffy mashed potato.

Sausage and Paprika One Pot

- Put the sausages on your browning tray and place on the high rack. Drizzle with a small amount of olive oil. Cook for 10 minutes at 220°C, before adding the onion, garlic and peppers. Continue to cook until browned, turning occasionally.
- Remove from the oven and place the sausages/onions in your casserole dish (making sure this fits well in your oven). Add the remaining ingredients apart from the spinach. Rinse out the tins of tomatoes and baked beans with a little water (about one-third of each tin) and add this to the mixture. Combine well.
- Pop on a lid or cover securely with a double layer of foil before placing on the low rack. Turn the temperature down to 200°C and cook for 25 minutes.
- Remove the lid and stir in the spinach leaves. Add more water or stock if you think it is necessary.
- Cook without a lid for another 10 minutes before serving with root mash. Delicious!

8–10 lean sausages
Olive oil
2 red onions, thickly sliced
3–4 cloves garlic, roughly chopped
2 red peppers, sliced
1 dessertspoon runny honey
1 tin chopped tomatoes
1 tin baked beans
1 tablespoon smoked paprika
Seasoning
2 handfuls of baby leaf spinach

Simple Coq au Vin

A quick and easy variation on the traditional French favourite.

4–6 chicken pieces
(breast or thigh,
whichever you
prefer)
Olive oil
Paprika
Seasoning
12 shallots, left whole
3–4 cloves garlic,
thickly sliced
200g smoked lardons
200g button
mushrooms
1 teaspoon butter
1 dessertspoon plain
flour or cornflour
500ml red wine
200ml port
2 bay leaves
2–3 sprigs of thyme

- Score the chicken pieces before rubbing with olive oil and sprinkling with paprika and seasoning.
- Drizzle a little olive oil in a deep ovenproof dish and add the chicken. Add the shallots, garlic and lardons and place on the high rack. Cook at 200°C for 15 minutes.
- Add the mushrooms and butter and cook for another 5–8 minutes, ensuring everything is combined.
- Remove from the oven. Remove the chicken and place to one side temporarily.
- Sprinkle the flour in the ovenproof dish to soak up any juices before adding a little of the wine, stirring to ensure it is combined. Then add the remaining wine and port.
- Add the bay leaves and thyme. Season well, before putting the chicken back in.
- Return to the halogen oven and cook for another 40–45 minutes.
- Serve with sauté or mashed potatoes and green vegetables.

Sweet Potato and Meatball Casserole

SERVES 4–6

- Place all the ingredients for the casserole in an ovenproof casserole dish (ensuring it fits well in your halogen) and season to taste. Cover with a lid or a double layer of tin foil securely fitted. Place the dish on the high rack. There needs to be space above the dish, so that it does not touch the element on the lid of the oven. If you are concerned, either use an extension ring or the lower rack. The benefit of using the high rack is that it allows more air to circulate all the way around the dish.
- Cook for 45 minutes at 210°C.
- Meanwhile, combine all the meatball ingredients together in a bowl and mix thoroughly.
- Form the mixture into small balls and place on a baking sheet. Cover the balls with a sheet of cling film and refrigerate for 20 minutes to rest.
- Then fry your meatballs in a sauté pan using a small amount of olive oil, until they are golden brown.
- Remove the lid from the casserole and add the meatballs. Check the liquid in the casserole – you may want to add more stock if it has evaporated. Combine well before popping the lid back on and cooking again for another 15–20 minutes, making sure the potato and carrots are tender.
- Serve with a sprinkle of parsley.

Note: You can freeze the meatballs raw. I normally place them, still on the baking tray, in the freezer until they are firm, before removing them from the tray and placing in a freezer bag. This way they won't stick together and you can pull out the required number of meatballs as and when you need them.

Casserole
2 large onions, finely chopped
2–3 cloves garlic, roughly chopped
2 carrots, diced
2 sticks of celery, diced
2 sweet potatoes, diced
1 tin chopped tomatoes
500ml vegetable stock
1 tablespoon paprika
2 bay leaves
Seasoning

Meatballs
400g beef mince
1 small onion, finely chopped or grated
1 teaspoon paprika
1 teaspoon cumin
1 chilli, finely chopped
1 teaspoon chilli powder
2 teaspoons Worcestershire sauce
1 teaspoon parsley
50g breadcrumbs
1 egg, beaten
Seasoning
Drizzle of olive oil

Parsley to serve

Beef and Mushroom in Red Wine

SERVES 4–6

500g stewing beef
   steak, cut into cubes
50g plain flour
3 teaspoons paprika
Olive oil
1 red onion, sliced
2 leeks, sliced
2 carrots, sliced
1 parsnip, sliced
2 tablespoons
   redcurrant jelly
200ml red wine
550ml beef stock
125g button
   mushrooms

- Place the beef steak in a bowl and coat with the flour and paprika.
- Select your ovenproof/hob-proof casserole dish, making sure it fits in your halogen oven. Place it on the hob and heat the oil over a medium heat. (If your casserole dish is not hob-proof, use a sauté pan and transfer into the casserole dish before placing in the halogen oven.)
- Add the onion and leeks to the olive oil and cook for 2 minutes.
- Add the beef and cook for a further 3–4 minutes, stirring well to avoid sticking.
- Add the carrots and parsnips and sweat for another 5 minutes with the lid on.
- Add the redcurrant jelly and stir well. Gradually add the wine and beef stock and button mushrooms. Continue to cook on the hob for another 15 minutes.
- Cover with a lid or a double layer of tin foil. Place the casserole on the low rack and cook for 1–1½ hours at 160°C. Check after 45 minutes as you may have to add more stock or water as it will evaporate.
- Serve with mashed potato for a comforting winter supper.

Beef Casserole with Stilton and Herb Dumplings

SERVES 4

- Place the flour and paprika in a bowl and season. Rinse the beef, then coat with the flour.
- Select your ovenproof/hob-proof casserole dish, making sure it fits in your halogen oven. Place this on the hob and heat a little oil over a medium heat.
- Add the beef and cook until browned. Then remove and leave to one side.
- Add the onion and garlic and cook until the onion starts to soften. Add the sweet potato and carrot and allow to sweat for a few minutes. Place the beef back in the casserole dish.
- Pour on the stout, stirring well. Then add the barley, sugar, bay leaves and thyme. Season to taste.
- Cook the casserole on the hob for another 5 minutes, before transferring to the low rack of the halogen oven. Cover with a lid or double layer of tin foil. Set the temperature to 160°C and cook for 50 minutes.
- Meanwhile, prepare the dumplings by mixing together the flour and suet. Then season and mix in the fresh parsley (if using) and crumbled stilton. Add a little water at a time until you have formed a pliable but not too sticky dough. Form into balls and leave on a floured surface until needed.
- Check the casserole after 50 minutes. Add the hot beef stock if needed. Cook again for 10 minutes, before removing the lid and adding the dumplings.
- Cook for a further 20–30 minutes until they are light and fluffy. Serve immediately.

3 tablespoons flour
1 tablespoon paprika
Seasoning
500g stewing beef
Olive oil
2 red onions, sliced
2 cloves garlic, roughly crushed
2 sweet potatoes, diced
4 carrots, diced
500ml stout
50g pearl barley
2 tablespoons brown sugar
2 bay leaves
Large handful of thyme, chopped

Dumplings
120g self-raising flour
50g suet
Seasoning
1 tablespoon fresh parsley (or 2 teaspoons dried)
50g stilton
3–4 tablespoons water

300–400ml hot beef stock

Lamb Hotpot

SERVES 4-6

400g lamb, cubed
50g plain flour
2–3 teaspoons paprika
Olive oil
3–4 leeks, sliced
2 cloves garlic,
   crushed
1–2 carrots, chopped
Knob of butter
500ml lamb stock
1 teaspoon mixed
   dried herbs
2–3 sprigs of fresh
   thyme (or cube of
   frozen fresh thyme)
6–8 potatoes, thinly
   sliced
25g mature Cheddar,
   grated

- In a bowl, mix the lamb with the flour and paprika, ensuring the lamb is evenly coated all over.
- On your hob, heat a little olive oil in a large sauté pan over a medium heat and fry the leeks and garlic for 2–3 minutes. Add the meat, carrots and butter and cook for a further 2–3 minutes to help brown the meat.
- Pour on the stock, dried herbs and thyme and cook for 10 minutes.
- Place a layer of potato slices in the bottom of a greased casserole dish – again make sure this fits in the halogen oven. Cover with a layer of meat mixture and continue alternating layers of meat and potato, finishing with a final layer of potato slices. Pop on a lid or cover securely with tin foil.
- Turn on the halogen oven to 210°C. Place the casserole dish on the low rack and cook for 45 minutes.
- Remove from the oven and sprinkle over the grated cheese before returning the hotpot without a lid for a final 20–30 minutes until the potatoes are tender.

Beef and Mushroom Cobbler

SERVES 4–6

- Place the beef steak in a bowl and coat with the flour and paprika.
- Select your ovenproof/hob-proof casserole dish, making sure it fits in your halogen oven. Place this on the hob and heat a little oil over a medium heat. (If your casserole dish is not hob-proof, use a sauté pan and transfer into the casserole dish before placing in the halogen oven.) Add the onion and leeks and cook for 5 minutes.
- Add the beef and cook for a further 5 minutes, stirring well to avoid sticking.
- Add the redcurrant jelly and stir well. Gradually add the wine and beef stock and button mushrooms. Cover and cook gently on a low heat for 20 minutes.
- Meanwhile, place the flour in a bowl. Add the yoghurt, oil and parsley. Mix to form a soft dough. Place on a floured board and shape into individual balls. Flatten slightly.
- Take the beef casserole off the hob, leaving it in the ovenproof casserole dish. Place the scones on the top of the casserole, forming a circle or completely covering the top.
- Place in the halogen on the low rack and set the temperature to 180°C. Bake for 20–30 minutes until the scones are golden and fluffy. Serve immediately.

450g stewing beef
   steak, cut into cubes
50g plain flour
3 teaspoons paprika
Olive oil
1 onion
2 leeks, sliced
2 tablespoons
   redcurrant jelly
200ml red wine
350mls beef stock
125g button
   mushrooms

Cobbler/scone mix
100g self–raising flour
75ml natural yoghurt
2 tablespoons olive oil
Small handful of
   parsley, chopped (or
   1 teaspoon dried
   parsley)

SERVES 4

500g lean stewing
   beef, diced
1 teaspoon ground
   ginger
1 teaspoon chilli
   powder
2 teaspoons paprika
Olive oil
1 red onion, finely
   sliced
2–3 cloves garlic,
   crushed
½–1 red chilli
   (depending on
   taste), finely
   chopped
1 red pepper, sliced
2 sticks of celery,
   sliced
1 small sweet potato,
   diced
1 tin chopped
   tomatoes
1 tin mixed beans,
   drained
250ml red wine
300ml beef stock
Seasoning to taste
2 handfuls of baby
   spinach leaves

Spicy Beef and Bean Casserole

A filling and very warming meal – serve with rice or taco shells.

- Place the beef in a bowl and add the ginger, chilli powder and paprika, ensuring it is evenly coated.
- Meanwhile, heat the olive oil over a medium heat in your hob-proof stock pot (which will transfer into the halogen later), or sauté pan if your stock pot is not hob-proof.
- Add the onion and garlic to the oil and cook for a couple of minutes before adding the beef to brown.
- Add the chilli and pepper and continue to cook for 5 minutes before removing from the heat.
- Add all remaining ingredients, apart from the spinach, to the stock pot. Cover with a lid or double layer of tin foil, secured well.
- Place on the high rack of your halogen. If this does not fit well, use an extension ring or place on the low rack. I prefer the high rack as it allows more heat to circulate all the way around the stock pot.
- Set the halogen to 170°C and cook for 1 hour. Then check the casserole to see if you need to add more stock or water. Turn the temperature up to 190°C and cook for another 15 minutes.
- Add the spinach leaves and combine well. Cook for another 5 minutes before serving.

Sweet and Creamy Lamb Curry

SERVES 4

This is a simple, slow-cook style lamb curry – a sort of cross between a curry and a casserole if I'm honest, but lovely. Feel free to make this as spicy or mild as you like. The recipe is mild to medium strength.

- In a bowl, mix the crushed coriander seeds, flour and seasoning. Dip in the lamb chunks, ensuring they are evenly coated.
- Heat the oil in a sauté pan on your hob over a medium heat. Add the lamb until browned. Then place in your casserole dish (making sure it fits into your halogen oven).
- Don't wash the sauté pan – add the onion, garlic, ginger and pepper and cook until they start to soften.
- Add the curry powder and cook for a minute or two before adding the chopped tomatoes. Cook for 2 minutes and then add to your casserole dish.
- Add the sultanas, apple, stock and half of the coriander leaves. Stir well, ensuring it is all combined. Cover and place on the high rack in the halogen at 180°C for 45 minutes.
- Remove the lid and check the tenderness of the lamb. Depending on the lamb you are cooking with, you may want to cook on a lower heat for slightly longer. You may need to add more stock or water the longer you cook as it may evaporate.
- When you are happy with the tenderness of the lamb, stir in the remaining coriander and crème fraîche. Cook for another 10 minutes.
- Serve on a bed of rice, garnished with chopped coriander leaves and a sprinkle of toasted almond slices.

1 teaspoon coriander seeds, crushed
50g flour
Seasoning to taste
500g lean lamb, diced
Olive oil
1 large red onion, finely sliced
3 cloves garlic, roughly chopped
4cm knuckle of ginger, finely chopped
1 pepper, finely diced
1 tablespoon sweet curry powder
1 tin chopped tomatoes
50g sultanas
1 dessert apple, peeled, cored and finely diced
300ml lamb stock (more may be necessary)
Handful of fresh coriander leaves, finely chopped
150ml crème fraîche

Chicken and Bacon with Wine and Tarragon Sauce

4–6 chicken thighs
Olive oil
Paprika
Seasoning
3–4 cloves garlic,
 lightly crushed
1 large red onion, cut
 into wedges
2 leeks, thickly sliced
100g thick bacon or
 lardons
2 carrots, cut into
 small sticks
Knob of butter
1 tablespoon flour
400ml chicken stock
300ml white wine
Handful of fresh
 tarragon
2 teaspoons
 wholegrain mustard
3–4 tablespoons crème
 fraîche
75g frozen peas,
 defrosted

This is a quick and easy variation on a long, slow-cook chicken casserole. Perfect if you are in a hurry but want the satisfying and comforting casserole.

- Score the top of the chicken thighs. Then rub with olive oil and sprinkle generously with paprika and seasoning.
- Place in a lightly oiled ovenproof dish (ideally a dish with sides as you will be adding to it later in the recipe). Scatter with the garlic, onion, leeks and bacon, ensuring everything is evenly distributed. Place on the high rack and cook for 20 minutes at 200°C.
- While the chicken is cooking, steam the carrots and heat the chicken stock.
- Remove the dish from the oven. Remove the chicken and place to one side for a few minutes. Add a little butter, which should melt with the heat of the pan. Add the flour and continue to stir with a wooden spoon, ensuring you are getting all the little bits of garlic and juices. Gradually add the hot chicken stock, stirring continually to avoid lumps. Add the white wine, tarragon, wholegrain mustard and season to taste. Stir in the crème fraîche, carrot and defrosted peas.
- Place the chicken back into the dish. Return to the halogen oven at the same temperature and cook for another 15–20 minutes.
- Once the chicken is cooked to your taste, remove from the oven. Garnish with tarragon and serve.

Pan-roasted Thai Chicken

SERVES 4

This is so simple yet seriously yummy. Ideally you need to marinate overnight or for at least 3 hours to really develop the flavours.

- If you have a food processor, this is really easy. Simply whizz all the ingredients, excluding the chicken, rice, peas and spring onions. If you don't have a processor, finely chop the vegetables and coriander.
- Place in a bowl or freezer bag and add the lime juice and olive oil. Then add the chicken pieces, cover or secure and leave to marinate.
- When you are ready to start cooking, tip the chicken into an oiled roasting pan, making sure it fits in your halogen oven.
- Turn the halogen on to 200°C and place the pan on the high rack. Cook for 20 minutes or until the chicken is cooked to your satisfaction.
- Meanwhile, cook your rice as per the manufacturer's instructions, adding the peas to the rice as they can be cooked together. When the rice is cooked, add the spring onions and combine.
- When you are ready to serve, place the chicken on a bed of rice. For added greenery, why not steam some mangetout, broccoli or pak choi.

2–3 cloves garlic
1 red onion
1 red chilli
2cm knuckle of ginger
1 lemongrass stalk, peeled
Small handful of coriander
Juice of 1 lime
1 tablespoon olive oil
4–6 chicken breasts, cut into thirds
300g basmati rice
75g peas
½ bunch of spring onions, finely chopped

Roasted Ratatouille Crumble

SERVES 4

2 red peppers, cut into
thick wedges

2 red onions, cut into
wedges

4–5 cloves garlic,
halved

8–10 tomatoes, scored
but left whole

1 small aubergine, cut
into thick wedges

2 courgettes, cut into
lengthways wedges

Olive oil

Balsamic vinegar

Sea salt

Sugar

Fresh thyme and
rosemary sprigs

2 tablespoons
breadcrumbs

2 tablespoons oats

1 tablespoon pumpkin
seeds

2 tablespoons
Parmesan cheese,
finely grated

Seasoning

1 jar of passata

Feta or goat's cheese,
crumbled (optional)

I love this dish. It can be made in advance or double up the recipe and freeze one as a crumble and keep the other as a normal ratatouille. For cheese addicts, you could add some crumbled feta or goat's cheese to the ratatouille before adding the crumble. Yummy!

- In an ovenproof dish, combine all the vegetables. Pour over a drizzle of olive oil, a dash of balsamic and a sprinkle of sea salt and sugar. Add the herb sprigs and toss again to ensure it is all evenly coated.
- Place on the high rack and cook at 200°C for 30 minutes.
- While that is cooking, combine the breadcrumbs, oats, pumpkin seeds and Parmesan. Season to taste.
- Remove the vegetables, add the passata and combine well. Season with black pepper. Add some crumbled feta or goat's cheese now, if you are a cheese addict!
- Cover with the crumble mix and place back in the oven for another 15 minutes.
- Serve immediately.

SUITABLE FOR VEGETARIANS

Simple Goulash

SERVES 4

- On your hob, brown the beef and onions in a little olive oil over a medium heat. I do this in my stock pot which is hob-proof as this saves me having to transfer into another dish. If you don't have a hob-proof stock pot that fits in your halogen, use a sauté pan and transfer once browned.
- When browned, add the remaining ingredients into your stock pot. Cover with a lid or double layer of tin foil, securely fastened. Place on the high rack of your halogen. (If your pot does not fit, use an extension ring or place on the low rack.)
- Cook at 180°C for 1 hour. Note that if you have chosen cheaper cuts of meat, which are ideal for slow cooking, I would advise that you reduce the temperature to 160°C and cook for 1½ hours. Remember to check the liquid as it may dry out a little and you may need to add a little extra water or stock. The slow cook process will help tenderise the meat.
- Serve with chopped parsley and a dollop of sour cream.

Olive oil
500g lean beef, diced
2 red onions, finely chopped
1 red pepper, finely chopped
2 tins chopped tomatoes or 700g fresh tomatoes, skinned and chopped
3 tablespoons paprika
Seasoning
Parsley and sour cream to serve

Lamb and Haricot Bean Casserole

SERVES 4

1 tablespoon flour
Seasoning
Lamb neck fillet, cut
  into chunks
1 red onion, finely
  chopped
2 cloves garlic,
  crushed
300ml red wine
300ml beef or chicken
  stock
1 tin tomatoes
2 sticks of celery,
  sliced
2 carrots, diced
1 tin haricot beans,
  drained
1–2 sprigs of rosemary,
  finely chopped

- Put the flour in a bowl and season to taste. Coat the lamb with the flour.
- On your hob, heat the oil in a sauté pan over a medium heat and then add the lamb. Cook until browned and then place the lamb into your casserole dish (making sure it fits into your halogen).
- Using the sauté pan with the remaining lamb juices, cook the onion and garlic until soft. Add this to the lamb. Return the pan to the heat and add the red wine and stock. Scrape up any browned bits of meat or onion and stir, before pouring this into your casserole dish.
- Add all of the remaining ingredients to the casserole and combine well. Cover with a lid or a double layer of foil, held securely.
- Place on the high rack in your halogen. If there is not enough room, use an extension ring or place on the lower rack.
- Cook at 180°C for 1 hour. Check the liquid as you may need to add more stock or wine. Continue to cook for another 30–45 minutes. The longer you cook, the more tender the lamb, but if you want to cook for over 1½ hours, reduce the temperature from the start to 160–170°C.
- Serve with mashed potato or mini roasties and green vegetables.

Italian-style Lamb

A satisfying one-pot dish that really hits the spot. Serve with crusty bread – delicious.

- On your hob, heat the oil in a sauté pan over a medium heat and brown the lamb. Then place it in the bottom of your casserole dish (making sure it fits in your halogen).
- Without cleaning the sauté pan, put the onion, garlic, pepper and celery into it and cook for 3–4 minutes to soften in the lamb juices. Pour over the wine, and scrape up any browned lamb from the bottom of the pan, ensuring it is all now in the liquid. Immediately transfer to the stock pot.
- Add all of the remaining ingredients to the pot, apart from the courgettes and Parmesan.
- Place in the halogen, ideally on the high rack if it fits. Alternatively, use an extension ring to raise the height of the element or place on the low rack. I prefer the high rack as I think it allows for better all-round cooking.
- Cook for 1 hour at 180°C. Check to see if you need more stock as it may evaporate. Once you are happy with the consistency, add the courgettes.
- Return and cook again for another 15–20 minutes or until the tenderness of the meat meets your requirements.
- Serve with a sprinkle of Parmesan.

SERVES 4

Olive oil
500g lean lamb, diced
2 red onions, finely chopped
3–4 cloves garlic, finely chopped
1 red pepper, diced
2 sticks of celery, diced
300ml red wine
1 tin chopped tomatoes
350ml lamb or vegetable stock
4–5 sundried tomatoes (in oil), drained and chopped
Handful of fresh herbs, chopped (ideally thyme, rosemary and oregano, but you can use basil)
Seasoning
2 courgettes, sliced
50g Parmesan cheese, grated

Spring Chicken

SERVES 4

Olive oil
Paprika
Seasoning
4 chicken breasts
3 leeks, thickly sliced
2–3 cloves garlic,
  roughly chopped
200g button
  mushrooms, halved
2 carrots, thickly sliced
4 tomatoes, cut into
  quarters
400ml hot chicken
  stock
250ml white wine or
  vermouth
2–3 sprigs of thyme
2–3 bay leaves

- Drizzle a little oil in a deep ovenproof dish. Rub the chicken with some more oil and then sprinkle with paprika and season to taste.
- Place on the high rack and cook for 15 minutes at 210°C until it starts to brown. Meanwhile, prepare the vegetables.
- Once the chicken has browned, remove from the oven and add the vegetables, ensuring they are evenly distributed.
- Combine the chicken stock and wine/vermouth and pour this over the chicken and vegetables. Finish with the sprigs of thyme and bay leaves. Cover with a double layer of foil, securely held.
- Place back in the oven and cook for another 30–40 minutes.
- When you are ready to serve, remove the bay leaves. Serve with fluffy mashed potato.

Lemon Chicken with Capers

This recipe would also work with pork.

- Place a little oil into a sauté pan on your hob over a medium heat. Add the chicken and brown off both sides for 5 minutes. Place the browned chicken in your ovenproof dish (making sure it fits in your halogen oven).
- Using the same sauté pan, cook the onion, garlic and celery until softened.
- Add 2–3 tablespoons of stock to the pan and sprinkle over the flour. Cook, stirring, for 1 minute.
- Gradually add the rest of the stock and the remaining ingredients, leaving half the parsley. Season to taste.
- Bring to the boil and pour over the chicken. Cover securely with a double layer of foil. Place on the high rack of the halogen, set the temperature to 200°C and cook for 45 minutes.
- Before serving, add the remaining parsley. Serve with potatoes or rice and green vegetables.

SERVES 4

Olive oil
1kg chicken thighs
2 onions, finely chopped
2 cloves garlic, roughly chopped
2 sticks of celery, diced
300ml chicken stock
1 tablespoon plain flour or cornflour
2 teaspoons lemon thyme, freshly chopped
Zest and juice of 1 lemon
300ml white wine
110g capers
2 tablespoons fresh parsley, chopped
Seasoning

Chicken and Bacon Casserole

SERVES 4

25g flour
Seasoning
300g chicken pieces
Olive oil
125g bacon, chopped
1 onion, finely
  chopped
2 cloves garlic,
  crushed (optional)
1 carrot, diced
2–3 sticks of celery,
  finely chopped
300ml chicken stock
100ml white wine
5 tomatoes, chopped
Small handful of fresh
  parsley, chopped

- Put the flour in a bowl and season. Then coat the chicken.
- On your hob, heat a little olive oil in a sauté pan over a medium heat and cook the chicken until it is browned. Remove the chicken and place it in your casserole dish (making sure it fits in your halogen).
- Add the bacon to the sauté pan, along with the onion and garlic. Cook until the bacon starts to brown and the onions soften. Add this to the casserole dish, with the carrot and celery.
- Then place the stock and white wine into the sauté pan. Heat this up and using a wooden spoon scrape up any cooked bits stuck to the pan. Pour all this into the casserole dish. Add the tomatoes and parsley. Combine well.
- Place the casserole dish on the high rack. (If the casserole dish is large, you may need to use an extension ring. Alternatively, place it on the lower rack, in which case you may need to cook for a little while longer.)
- Set the temperature to 190°C and cook for 50–60 minutes.
- Serve with green vegetables and mash or new potatoes.

Vegetable and Lentil Caserole

SERVES 4–6

- Using a hobproof/ovenproof dish, cook the onion, garlic and red pepper on the hob in a little olive oil.
- Add the celery, leek and potatoes and sweat for 5–8 minutes. Add all the remaining ingredients and season to taste.
- Allow to simmer for 10 minutes before transferring to your halogen oven.
- Cover with a lid or double layer of tin foil.
- Place the casserole dish on the high rack (if the casserole dish is large you may need to use an extension ring, or if not, place on the lower rack but you may need to cook for a while longer). Cook at 190°C for 45 minutes.
- Remove and serve immediately.

Olive oil
1 onion, finely chopped
2 cloves garlic, crushed
1 red pepper, diced
2 sticks celery, diced
1 leek, diced
2 sweet potatoes, peeled and diced
6–8 new potatoes, quartered
1 tin chopped tomatoes
400ml vegetable stock
75g red lentils
1 bay leaf
1 dessertspoon of chopped parsley
1 teaspoon dried Italian herbs
Seasoning to taste

SUITABLE FOR VEGETARIANS

Pies and Savoury Crumbles

This is a real comfort food chapter – a variety of pies and crumbles that will fill you up and give you that metaphoric hug when you are feeling low. Most of these recipes can be prepared in advance, so that they are there ready to be popped in the oven when you are ready to cook.

Beef, Chocolate Stout and Chilli Pie

SERVES 4–6

2 dessertspoons
   paprika
2 dessertspoons flour
Seasoning
1kg lean braising steak
25g butter
1 large red onion,
   finely chopped
2–3 cloves garlic,
   crushed
½–1 red chilli, finely
   chopped
500ml chocolate stout
3 beef stock cubes
   (depending on
   desired thickness of
   gravy), dissolved in
   300ml of hot water
½ sheet of ready-rolled
   puff pastry
1 egg, beaten

*I use chocolate stout in this
pie as it goes brilliantly
with the beef. If you can't
get hold of chocolate stout,
use ordinary stout and add
a dessertspoon of cocoa to it.
As with most recipes using
braising steak, the meat is
better and more tender when
left to cook slowly.*

- Place the paprika and flour in a large freezer bag and season to taste. Add the braising steak and shake until evenly covered.
- On your hob, heat the butter in a deep sauté or stock pot over a medium heat and add the floured beef. Cook until browned.
- Add the onion, garlic and chilli and allow to sweat for 5 minutes before adding the stout.
- Once the ale is combined with all the juices and vegetables, add the stock.
- Leave to cook slowly on a low/medium heat for 1 hour. If the mixture becomes too dry, add a little more water. (If you prefer to use the halogen at this point instead of the hob, decant into a deep ovenproof pie dish, cover with foil and cook at 160°C for 1 hour on the low rack, checking half way through to see if it needs more water added.)
- Place the beef into your deep ovenproof pie dish.
- Roll out your pastry – ideally to an approximately 4–5mm thickness.
- Brush the edges of the dish with beaten egg and place the pastry over the top of the pie. Crimp the edges to seal and coat the top with the egg as this helps to give it a nice golden colour. You will probably have some pastry left over – if you are feeling creative, you could cut out some leaf shapes and decorate the top of the pie.
- Place the pie on the high rack. Cook for 30–40 minutes at 200°C until golden and the pastry has puffed and cooked thoroughly.
- Serve immediately with mashed potato and greens.

Cowboy's Pie

Kids love this – a variation on the cottage pie.

- Place the potatoes and carrots in a steamer or boil until soft.
- Meanwhile, on your hob heat the oil in a large sauté pan over a medium heat and fry the onion for 3–4 minutes. Then add the mince.
- Cook until brown, before adding the baked beans and chopped tomatoes.
- Cook for 10 minutes until tender and reduced to the desired consistency. Add more stock or water if you prefer a more liquid base. Season to taste and add a splash of Worcestershire sauce.
- Mash the steamed potato and carrots together. Add the butter and two-thirds of the Cheddar. Mix thoroughly.
- Place the mince in a deep ovenproof dish and spoon the mash over the top. Be careful not to overfill the dish. Press the mash down gently with a fork. Top with the remaining grated cheese and a sprinkle of paprika.
- Place on the low rack and cook for 20–25 minutes at 200°C.

400g potato, cut into rough chunks
400g sweet potato, cut into chunks
1–2 carrots, cut into chunks
Spray of olive oil
1 onion, chopped
400g lean mince (or pre-drained of fat)
1 tin baked beans
1 tin chopped tomatoes
Seasoning
Worcestershire sauce
25g butter
75g mature Cheddar
Paprika

Shepherd's Pie

This is always a family favourite.

SERVES 4

800g potato, cut into
rough chunks
4 carrots, 2 cut into
small cubes, 2
roughly chopped
1 onion, chopped
400g lean lamb mince
50g mushrooms, sliced
(optional)
100ml red wine
1 teaspoon yeast
extract (Marmite or
similar)
200ml hot lamb or
beef stock
Seasoning
25g butter
75g mature Cheddar
Paprika

- Place the potato and the chopped carrots in a steamer or boil until soft.
- Meanwhile, in a large sauté pan on your hob, cook the onion for 3–4 minutes over a medium heat before adding the mince. Cook until brown and then add the cubed carrots, mushrooms and wine.
- Dissolve the yeast extract in the hot stock before adding to the mince. Cook for 20 minutes until tender and reduced to your desired consistency. Season to taste.
- Mash the potato and carrots together. Add the butter and two-thirds of the Cheddar. Mix thoroughly.
- Place the mince in a deep ovenproof baking dish, making sure it fits well into your halogen oven. Pipe or smooth the mash on the top, taking care not to overfill. Press down gently with a fork and top with the remaining grated cheese and a sprinkle of paprika.
- Place on the low rack and bake for 20–30 minutes at 180°C.

Creamy Haddock Pie with Crisp Rosti Topping

- Boil the potatoes for 10 minutes. They should still be firmish, not completely cooked. Drain and leave to one side to cool. Note that you also need to hardboil the eggs – I cheat by boiling them with the potatoes, making sure I only cook them for 6–7 minutes.
- Meanwhile, into another saucepan, put the milk, bay leaf, black pepper to taste and haddock pieces. Bring to the boil and cook for 10 minutes, or until the fish is cooked (it should flake easily).
- Then drain the fish, retaining the milk for later. Remove the bay leaf and discard. You can reuse the saucepan, so no need to wash up!
- In the saucepan, melt 1 dessertspoon butter and add the flour to form a paste. Gradually add the warm milk until you form a smooth sauce. Continue to stir well until it starts to thicken. If you get any lumps, switch to a balloon whisk and beat well.
- Add the mustard and season to taste. Stir in the parsley.
- Place the fish in the bottom of an ovenproof dish (making sure it fits in your halogen). Chop the boiled eggs and add to the dish. Pour on the sauce and combine well.
- Grate the potatoes with a coarse grater. Melt 50g butter and combine with the potatoes. Season to taste. Spoon this over the fish. Finish with a sprinkle of Parmesan and a sprinkle of breadcrumbs.
- When you are ready to cook, place the dish on the high rack. Set the temperature to 200°C and cook for 25 minutes until golden.

600g potato
4 eggs
400ml milk
1 bay leaf
Black pepper
450g haddock
1 dessertspoon butter
1 dessertspoon flour
2 teaspoons
  wholegrain mustard
Small handful of fresh
  parsley, chopped
50g butter
50g Parmesan
50g breadcrumbs

Leek, Mushroom and Stilton Pie

SERVES 4–6

2–3 leeks, finely
   chopped
150g button or
   chestnut
   mushrooms, halved
   if chestnut
300ml single cream
175g Stilton or blue
   cheese
Black pepper
Nutmeg
30g toasted pine nuts
8–10 sheets filo pastry
Approx 25g butter,
   melted
2–3 large handfuls of
   baby leaf spinach
2–3 dessertspoons
   cranberry sauce

SUITABLE FOR VEGETARIANS

- In a deep sauté pan over a medium heat, fry/sweat the leeks in a little butter. Once they are starting to soften, add the mushrooms and cook until soft but not soggy.
- Turn the heat to low/medium and add the cream and Stilton. Season with black pepper and nutmeg and then add the pine nuts, reserving a small handful for later.
- Line a greased flan dish with 3–4 sheets of filo, overlapping to avoid any gaps and brushing with butter in between each sheet to help them stick. Leave the edges hanging over, as they can be used to form part of the top later.
- Pour the leek mixture into the flan dish. Smooth out and then add a layer of spinach leaves. Finish with random dollops of the cranberry sauce.
- Bring across the edges to help form the top. Cut any remaining sheets of filo into manageable squares, brush with melted butter, scrunch up and place in the gaps on the top of the pie. Continue until you fill the top with roughly scrunched up filo. Sprinkle with the remaining pine nuts.
- Either freeze until needed or bake. Place on the low rack and cook at 200°C for 40 minutes until golden all over. If the top starts to get too dark before the pie is cooked through, use the extension ring to lift the element away from the pie, or cover gently with some tin foil.
- Serve with a lovely salad, or you can even serve with roast potatoes and vegetables. Rich but delicious.

Simple Chicken, Mushroom and Bacon Filo Pie

This is a very simple recipe, which looks far more impressive than it really is. Cook it in advance for an effortless meal.

- In a sauté pan on your hob, heat a little olive oil over a medium heat. Add the chicken pieces and cook until they start to brown. Add the bacon, onion and mushroom and continue to cook for another 5 minutes.
- Add the cream cheese and milk, and stir well until it forms a creamy sauce. If you like a really creamy taste, you could add a dollop or two of crème fraîche or natural Greek yoghurt.
- Add the thyme and season to taste before removing from the heat. Pour the mixture into a deep pie dish. (I use a deep-sided ovenproof dish.)
- Melt the butter in a saucepan. Cut the filo pastry sheets in half and brush each sheet very roughly with the melted butter. Scrunch up roughly/loosely and place randomly on the top of the chicken mixture. Continue until it is covered but don't over load the top with tightly packed bundles of pastry, just make sure it is covered. Finish with a sprinkle of sesame seeds and a dash of black pepper.
- Place the pie on the high rack and set the temperature to 210°C. Cook for 20–30 minutes until golden and bubbly.
- Serve with mashed potato and seasonal vegetables.

SERVES 4–6

Olive oil
400g boneless chicken pieces, diced
8 rashers lean bacon, diced
1 red onion, diced
175g button mushrooms, halved
1 x 350g tub cream cheese
200ml milk
Crème fraîche or natural Greek yoghurt (optional)
2–3 sprigs of thyme, finely chopped
Seasoning
30g butter
½ pack filo pastry
15g sesame seeds

SERVES 4–6

2 dessertspoons
   paprika
2 dessertspoons flour
Seasoning
25g butter
1kg lean braising steak
1 large red onion,
   finely chopped
2–3 cloves garlic,
   crushed
75g button
   mushrooms
2 small carrots, diced
500ml real ale
3–4 beef stock cubes
   (depending on
   desired thickness of
   gravy), dissolved in
   300ml hot water
Small handful of fresh
   thyme
1 egg, beaten
½ sheet ready-rolled
   puff pastry

Steak and Ale Pie

This is best I think if you use a traditional real ale, but I will leave that up to you. As with most recipes using braising steak, the meat is better and more tender when left to cook slowly. You can do this in the halogen oven or on the hob, whatever you find easier.

• Place the paprika and flour in a large freezer bag and season to taste. Add the braising steak and shake until evenly covered.
• On your hob, heat the butter in a deep sauté or stock pot over a medium heat and add the floured beef. Cook until browned.
• Add the onion, garlic, mushrooms and carrots and allow to sweat for 5 minutes. Then add the ale.
• Once the ale is combined with all the juices and vegetables, add the stock and thyme.
• Leave to cook slowly on a low/medium heat for 1 hour. If the mixture becomes too dry, add a little more water. (If you prefer to use the halogen at this point instead of the hob, decant into your deep ovenproof pie dish, cover with foil and cook at 160°C for 1 hour on the low rack, checking halfway through to see if it needs more liquid added.)
• Place the beef into your deep ovenproof pie dish. Brush the edges of the dish with beaten egg and place the pastry over the top of the pie. Crimp the edges to seal and coat the top with egg as this helps give it a nice golden colour.
• Place the pie on the high rack and set the halogen to 200°C. Cook for 30 minutes until golden.
• Serve immediately with mashed potato and greens.

Creamy Chicken Crumble

This is actually really simple to make and can be made in advance ready to pop in the halogen. If you like a cheesy crust to your crumble, simply add 30–50g of grated mature Cheddar or Parmesan to the crumble mixture.

- In your sauté pan (or use your hob-proof oven dish to save washing up), heat a little olive oil over a medium heat. Add the butter and leeks and cook for 5 minutes.
- Add the mushrooms and garlic and cook for another few minutes before adding the chicken.
- Once the chicken is warmed through, add the cream cheese and milk, stirring to form a creamy sauce. (If you want a creamier sauce, you can add a dollop or two of crème fraîche or natural Greek yoghurt).
- Add the thyme and season to taste. Then remove from the heat. Transfer into your ovenproof dish if you are not already using one.
- Place the flour and butter into a bowl. Rub with your fingertips until you form a crumble (which has a look similar to breadcrumbs). Mix in the breadcrumbs, oats and seeds and season to taste. If you are using cheese, add this now.
- Sprinkle this over the creamy chicken mixture, ensuring it is all covered.
- Place on the high rack and cook for 20–25 minutes at 200°C until golden.
- Serve with seasonal green salad.

SERVES 4

Olive oil
25g butter
2–3 leeks, finely sliced
75g button mushrooms, halved or whole
2–3 cloves garlic, crushed
400g chicken, cooked roughly chopped
1 tub cream cheese
200ml milk
Crème fraîche or natural Greek yoghurt (optional)
1 teaspoon dried thyme
Seasoning

Crumble
100g wholemeal flour
50g butter
75g wholemeal breadcrumbs
75g oats
75g mixed seeds
50g mature Cheddar or Parmesan, grated (optional)

Simple Mixed Bean and Vegetable Crumble

SERVES 4

Olive oil
1 large red onion,
  finely sliced
3 cloves garlic, crushed
1 red pepper, diced
2 sticks of celery, diced
1 carrot, diced
1 small sweet potato,
  diced
1 tin mixed beans,
  drained
1 tin chopped tomatoes
2 teaspoons sundried
  tomato purée
200ml red wine or
  vegetable stock
1 tablespoon fresh
  thyme, chopped
1 tablespoon fresh
  marjoram, chopped
Seasoning

Crumble
100g wholemeal flour
50g butter
75g oats
75g wholemeal
  breadcrumbs
50g mixed seeds
50g Parmesan cheese,
  grated

• Drizzle oil into a saucepan or your ovenproof casserole dish and place on the hob over a medium heat. Add the onion, garlic and pepper and cook until they start to soften.
• Add the celery, carrot and sweet potato and sweat for 5 minutes. Then add all the remaining ingredients apart from those for the crumble.
• Cook for 10–12 minutes and then remove from the heat.
• Into a bowl, place the wholemeal flour and butter. Rub until you form a texture similar to breadcrumbs. Add the oats, breadcrumbs, seeds and Parmesan and season well.
• Cover the vegetable mixture with the crumble mix until evenly coated.
• Turn the halogen oven on to 200°C and place the crumble on the high rack. Cook for 25–30 minutes until golden and bubbling.
• Serve immediately with a green salad.

SUITABLE FOR VEGETARIANS

Creamy Fish Crumble

- Place the fish and milk in a pan on your hob and bring the milk to the boil. Reduce the heat and cook gently for 10 minutes or until the fish is cooked through.
- Drain the fish, reserving the liquid for making the sauce. Shred the fish and place in your ovenproof dish.
- To make a creamy sauce, melt the butter in a pan and add the flour. Stir in the reserved milk stock and heat gently until the sauce thickens. I normally use a whisk at this stage as it helps prevent any lumps from forming. Stir continuously. Add the mustard and season to taste.
- Pour the sauce over the fish.
- Into a bowl, place the wholemeal flour and the butter. Rub until you form a texture similar to breadcrumbs. Add the oats, breadcrumbs, seeds and Parmesan and season well.
- Cover the fish with the crumble mix until evenly coated.
- Turn the halogen oven on to 200°C and place the crumble on the high rack. Cook for 25–30 minutes until golden and bubbling.
- Serve immediately with a green salad.

500g fish fillets or ask your fishmonger for pieces of flaky white fish
200g salmon pieces (optional)
100g prawns (optional)
250ml milk
25g butter
25g flour
1 teaspoon mustard
Seasoning

Crumble
100g wholemeal flour
50g butter
75g oats
75g wholemeal breadcrumbs
50g mixed seeds (optional)
50g Parmesan cheese, grated

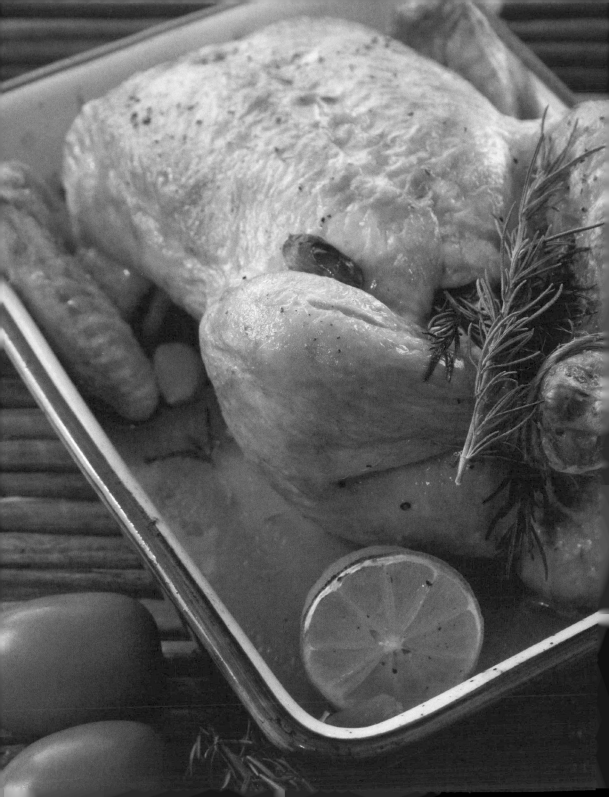

Complete Meals

In speaking to people about how they use their halogen oven, the one thing they often tell me they struggle with is how to use it for making a complete meal. Hopefully my other books have helped with this, but this chapter should dispel any remaining doubts.

4–6 large potatoes
250g Chantenay
  carrots
1 head of broccoli
Olive oil
1 teaspoon sugar
Seasoning
2 tablespoons
  semolina
½–1 tablespoon
  paprika
2–3 red onions, halved
1 small/medium
  whole chicken
1 lemon
30g butter
1–2 teaspoons dried or
  fresh thyme

Gravy
1 tablespoon plain
  flour
250ml red wine
Seasoning
Dash of yeast extract
  (optional)
Fresh chicken stock,
  heated

Roast Chicken, Roast Potatoes with Glazed Carrots and Broccoli Florets

You may need the extension ring to make this meal.

- Prepare your potatoes and steam or boil them for 10–15 minutes.
- Meanwhile, prepare your vegetable parcels. Evenly cut the carrots lengthways and cut the broccoli into florets. Cut two lengths of tin foil. Place your carrots in the centre of one (ensuring the piece of foil is big enough to seal) and the broccoli in the centre of the other. Put 1 tablespoon of olive oil, the sugar and 2 tablespoons of water in with the carrots. Season to taste and seal securely. Put 2–3 tablespoons of water in with the broccoli, season to taste and seal securely. Leave to one side.
- Turn the halogen oven on to 230°C and remove all trays. Pour a few tablespoons of olive oil in the base of the halogen bowl. Leave to heat while you move to the next step.
- Drain your potatoes and place them back into the empty saucepan. Add the semolina and paprika. Replace the lid and shake thoroughly.
- Place the potatoes and 2 halved red onions in the halogen bowl, carefully, so you are not splashed with the oil. Using tongs, turn the potatoes so they are coated in the oil. Cook for 10 minutes while you get on with the chicken.
- Wash and prepare your chicken according to your own preference. I place 1 whole red onion and 1 lemon, both cut in half, in the cavity of the bird to

enhance the flavour. I then rub the skin with butter and sprinkle with thyme. You could also smear herb butter under the skin.

- Remove the potatoes and place on a dish, covered with foil. Leave to one side. Leave the oil in the bowl as the chicken juices will run into it and you can use this at a later stage to make the gravy. Place the chicken, breast-side down, on the lower rack, drizzle with a little olive oil and cook for 25 minutes.

- Turn the chicken back over so the breast-side is up, add the potatoes around the edges of the chicken, reduce the temperature to 210°C and cook for another 20 minutes. Add the vegetable parcels. You may need to use the extension ring if you do not have room (you must keep at least 5cm from the element).

- Cook for another 15–25 minutes until the chicken and vegetables are cooked to your satisfaction. The timings obviously depend on the size of the bird and how you prefer your vegetables. As with all meat, make sure it is thoroughly cooked before eating.

- The fat will have drained to the base of the halogen oven. You can use some of this juice to make your gravy.

- To make a quick gravy: place the leftover juice into a saucepan on your hob over a medium heat. Add the plain flour and stir with a wooden spoon until combined. Add the red wine and seasoning (add a dash of yeast extract if you like the flavour). Allow this to cook for a few minutes to reduce. Add fresh chicken stock (ideally hot) and continue to stir until you reach your desired consistency. Serve immediately.

Oven-roasted Italian-style Chicken with Crispy Potatoes

SERVES 4

1kg new potatoes,
  washed
4 chicken breasts
1 small pot cream
  cheese
2–3 cloves garlic,
  crushed
Small handful of fresh
  basil leaves (or 1
  teaspoon dried basil)
Seasoning
1 small pack pancetta
100g cherry tomatoes
1–2 red onions,
  quartered
1–2 red peppers,
  deseeded and thickly
  sliced
2–3 cloves garlic,
  roughly chopped
Olive oil
Balsamic vinegar
Sprigs of fresh thyme
  and rosemary
1 teaspoon paprika

- Boil or steam the potatoes for 10–15 minutes until they are soft but not so soft they break apart.
- Meanwhile, cut two-thirds into the chicken breast to form a pocket. Mix the cream cheese, garlic and basil together. Season to taste and stuff each chicken breast with 1–2 teaspoons of the mixture.
- Wrap the pancetta around the chicken breasts securely and place on a greased ovenproof dish or roasting tin, making sure this fits well in your halogen oven. If possible, choose a dish that is large enough for you to place the potatoes in later.
- Add the tomatoes, red onion, peppers and garlic to your dish or roasting pan alongside the chicken. Drizzle with olive oil and a touch of balsamic vinegar and add the fresh herbs (reserving a little thyme for your potatoes). Season to taste. If there is any pancetta left, you can dice this and add to the mix.
- Place on the high rack and cook at 200°C for 10 minutes.
- Drain the potatoes and place them on a flat surface. Carefully using a potato masher, gently press down just enough so the potatoes break open. Drizzle with a little olive oil and a sprinkle of paprika and thyme.
- Add these to your ovenproof dish. If your dish is too small for the potatoes, you can place the chicken on the high rack and potatoes on the low rack and swap them around halfway through this final stage of cooking. Hopefully you will have room.
- Place back on the rack and cook for another 15–20 minutes until the chicken is cooked to perfection. Serve immediately.

Roast Leg of Lamb with Roasted Vegetables

- Mix together the garlic, chilli, rosemary, seasoning and olive oil to form a paste. Rub this over the leg of lamb. You can score the flesh first to help give the paste something to hold on to. Place on the lower rack and cook for 15 minutes at 230°C.
- Meanwhile, cut the potatoes to size and steam or parboil for 10 minutes. Drain and return to the empty saucepan. Add the paprika and semolina. Pop the lid back on the saucepan and shake to fluff up and coat the vegetables.
- Place the potatoes around the lamb. Spray with olive oil. Halve the onions and place them with the vegetables, along with the rosemary sprigs.
- Cook for another 10 minutes before turning down to 190°C and cooking for 30–45 minutes or until both the meat and potatoes are cooked to your satisfaction. The cooking time for lamb depends on the size of the joint. Remember to turn the lamb and vegetables regularly and add a spray of oil or paste as required.
- Serve with homemade gravy.

3–4 cloves garlic, crushed
½ teaspoon chopped chillies
1 teaspoon dried rosemary
Seasoning
2–3 tablespoons olive oil
1 leg of lamb
2 sweet potatoes
6–8 potatoes
2–3 teaspoons paprika
2–3 teaspoons semolina
Olive oil spray
2 red onions
2–3 sprigs of rosemary

Chicken Burgers, Potato Wedges and Salad

SERVES 4

Chicken burgers
1 onion, chopped
1–2 cloves garlic, crushed
1 stick of celery, chopped
½ yellow pepper, chopped
500g chicken mince
30g pine nuts
1 tablespoon home-prepared wholemeal breadcrumbs

3–5 large potatoes, cut into wedges
Olive oil
Paprika
Seasoning
Seasonal salad produce
Tomatoes
4 wholemeal baps
Mayonnaise

- Place all of the chicken burger ingredients in a food processor and mix thoroughly.
- When mixed, form into balls – they should be firm but moist. If the mixture is dry, add some beaten egg. Use the palm of your hand to flatten the balls into burger shapes. You can refrigerate them until you are ready to cook, or freeze them in layers (separate each layer with parchment to prevent them from sticking together).
- Meanwhile, cut the unpeeled potatoes into wedges.
- Spray your baking tray with olive oil. Add the potato wedges and spray them lightly. Then sprinkle with paprika and seasoning. If you like flavours, you could add some potato wedge flavouring, available in packets from supermarkets, but don't use too much as it can be quite powdery and overpowering.
- Place the potatoes on the high rack and set the halogen to 200°C. Cook for 20–30 minutes, turning occasionally.
- When you are ready to cook the burgers, brush them lightly with olive oil. Turn the halogen up to 250°C and move the potato wedges on the base or low rack. Place the chicken burgers on the grill rack and cook them for 4–5 minutes on each side until golden. (See the section on Grilling in Chapter 1 for tips.)
- Meanwhile make a salad, using seasonal salad produce. Leave some lettuce leaves and slices of tomato to go in each bap.
- Place the wedges on your serving dish and the burgers in the bap. Add some mayonnaise, lettuce and tomato slices to each bap before closing.

Toad in the Hole with Mini Roasted Potatoes

- Parboil or steam the potatoes for 10 minutes.
- Using a blender with a balloon whisk, blend the flour, milk and egg together to form a batter. Leave to settle.
- Meanwhile, place the onion, sausages and a drizzle of olive oil in an ovenproof dish that fits well in your halogen. Drain the potatoes and place in the dish. Finish with a spray of oil and a sprinkle of paprika to help colour and flavour.
- Place on the high rack and cook for 10 minutes at 230°C, turning occasionally.
- Just before the 10 minutes are up, give the batter mix a quick whizz with your balloon whisk, adding the herbs and seasoning before a final whizz.
- Remove the dish from the oven and turn the heat down to 200°C.
- Remove the potatoes and place these on an oiled tray on the low rack (you can place them directly on the base of the oven if this suits you better). Whilst the sausages are still very hot, pour over the batter, ensuring that all the sausages are covered.
- Return the toad in the hole to the oven and cook on the high rack for 25–30 minutes until golden. If the sausages brown before the potatoes, swap them over so that the potatoes are on the high rack and the toad in the hole is on the lower rack.
- Serve with onion gravy and steamed vegetables.

500–750g potatoes, cut into 5cm chunks
100g plain flour
300ml milk
1 egg
1 onion, chopped
8 lean sausages
Olive oil
Paprika
Handful of fresh herbs such as thyme, oregano, rosemary, or 2 teaspoons of dried herbs
Seasoning

Stilton Pork Chops with Roasted New Potatoes

SERVES 4

1kg new potatoes, washed

Olive oil

3 sprigs of rosemary

2 teaspoons paprika

2–3 cloves garlic, roughly chopped

4 pork chops

75–100g Stilton or blue cheese, crumbled

Seasoning

- Place the new potatoes in a bowl, drizzle with olive oil and add the rosemary, paprika and garlic. Combine well, ensuring the potatoes are evenly coated in the oil. Place on an oiled browning tray and pop on the high rack for 30–40 minutes at 200°C, turning occasionally.
- When the potatoes are almost ready, place them on the low rack or base of the halogen. Oil the pork chops and then place them on the grilling rack and turn the halogen to the high grill setting. (See the section on grilling in Chapter 1 for tips.)
- Cook on each side until done to your desired taste – this should take about 5–8 minutes each side.
- Once cooked, crumble the Stilton over the chops, season to taste and return to grill for another 3–4 minutes until the Stilton is golden and bubbly.
- Remove the chops and new potatoes from the oven and serve with green vegetables.

Stuffed Tomatoes with Rocket and Parmesan Salad

This is a really lovely meal, especially on a summer's evening. You need to prepare it about an hour in advance of the cooking time at least. Ideal if you want to prepare something in advance and enjoy the rest of the time with your friends.

- Place the rice in a bowl and add the wine.
- Carefully cut the top off the tomatoes and reserve them for later. Then scoop out the flesh, again leaving the tomato cases to one side.
- Place the tomato flesh in with the rice. Add the spring onion, garlic, red pepper, sundried tomatoes and chopped basil. Season well. Leave for 1 hour for the rice to absorb the liquid.
- Fill the tomatoes with the mixture and place the tomato lids on top. Place in an oiled ovenproof dish, drizzle with a little oil and a sprinkle of sea salt. Place on the high rack for 25–30 minutes at 200°C.
- Just before serving, prepare the salad by placing the rocket in a dish. Combine with the spring onions and finish with the Parmesan slivers. When serving, drizzle with balsamic and olive oil. This is also delicious served with a lovely new potato salad.

50g risotto rice
200ml white wine
4 large tomatoes
2–3 spring onions, finely chopped
2–3 cloves garlic, crushed
½ red pepper, finely chopped
2–3 sundried tomatoes (in oil), drained and finely chopped
Small handful of basil, freshly chopped
Seasoning
1 bag washed rocket
3 spring onions, finely chopped
Slivers of Parmesan
Balsamic vinegar
Olive oil

SUITABLE FOR VEGETARIANS

Grilled Steak and Chunky Chips

SERVES 4

3–4 large potatoes
Olive oil spray
Paprika (optional)
3–4 sirloin steaks
2–3 cloves garlic
Dash of olive oil
Black pepper
Sea salt
Malt vinegar

- Slice the potatoes into chips and and place them in a bowl of water for a few minutes. Drain and then steam or boil for 5 minutes.
- Meanwhile, spray your baking tray with olive oil. I use the browning tray as it helps brown the potato chips.
- Drain the potatoes and place on the baking tray in a single layer. Spray with a little more olive oil and sprinkle with paprika. (This is optional but helps to create a golden colour and nice flavour.)
- Place on the high rack and bake for 15 minutes at 200°C. Then turn over, spray again and cook for another 10 minutes.
- Meanwhile, prepare your steaks as you would normally do. I rub mine with garlic and olive oil and season with black pepper.
- Move the chips onto the low rack and place the steak on the grill rack, either directly on the rack or on the browning plate if you have one (see the section on grilling in Chapter 1 for tips).
- Reset the temperature to 240°C and cook for 8–10 minutes. You can reduce or increase the temperature depending on how you like your steak done – this timing is perfect for a medium/rare 2–3cm thick steak.
- Remove the steak and leave to rest. Move the chips back up to the high rack. Turn the temperature down to 220°C and continue to cook the chips until golden – they should only take about another 5 minutes depending on the thickness of the chips.
- Serve with a lovely salad. Sprinkle the chips with sea salt and malt vinegar before serving.

One-pot Pork with Rosemary and Garlic Potatoes

- Wash the potatoes and cut them in half. Then boil or steam them for 8 minutes.
- Drizzle a little olive oil into an ovenproof dish. Add the tomatoes, onion, pepper, garlic and rosemary. Toss well in the oil, ensuring everything is evenly covered. Season to taste with sea salt and black pepper.
- Layer potatoes and tomatoes in the dish.
- Rub the chops with olive oil and place amongst the vegetables.
- Cover the dish with a lid or double layer of tin foil, held securely. Place on the high rack for 30 minutes at 200°C.
- Remove the cover and cook for another 10–20 minutes until the chops and potatoes have browned.
- Serve with green vegetables.

750g new potatoes
Olive oil
450g cherry tomatoes, left whole
1 red onion, thickly sliced or wedged
1 red pepper, thickly sliced
5–6 cloves garlic, whole or halved
4 sprigs of rosemary
Seasoning
4 pork loin chops

Cider Chicken with Roasted New Potatoes

SERVES 4

1kg new potatoes, washed
Olive oil
3 sprigs of rosemary
2 teaspoons paprika
2–3 cloves garlic, roughly chopped
4 boneless chicken breasts
25g butter
2 leeks, finely sliced
175g button mushrooms
300ml dry cider
200ml chicken stock
1 teaspoon dried thyme
Seasoning

- Place the new potatoes in a bowl, drizzle with olive oil and add the rosemary, paprika and garlic. Combine well to ensure the potatoes are evenly coated in the oil.
- Place the potatoes on an oiled browning tray on the high rack. Cook for 10–12 minutes at 200°C (basically until your chicken is ready for the oven) while you get on with the chicken dish.
- On your hob, heat a little oil in a sauté pan over a medium heat and cook the chicken until browned. Then place the chicken in a shallow ovenproof dish while you continue with the rest of the dish.
- Put the butter into the sauté pan followed by the leeks and mushrooms. Cook on the hob over a medium heat until they start to soften.
- Pour in the cider and stock, add the thyme and season to taste. Cook for another 3 minutes until heated thoroughly. Then place in the shallow ovenproof dish along with the chicken breasts. Cover with a double layer of tin foil, securely held.
- Remove the potatoes from the high rack. Turn them to help cook evenly. Place the chicken dish on the high rack and the potatoes on the low rack (you may want to use the extension ring to give you more room if your dish is quite deep). Cook for another 20–25 minutes until the potatoes and chicken are cooked.
- Serve with green vegetables.

Garlicky Chicken with Roasted New Potatoes

SERVES 4

This dish really is garlicky, so if you don't like garlic, avoid it. You can use whatever chicken pieces you prefer. I like chicken breasts. Prepare this up to a day in advance to allow the flavours to really develop.

- Using a food processor or electric mini chopping gadget, whizz the garlic cloves, olive oil, lemon juice and zest together until they form a smooth creamy paste. Add the crème fraîche and mustard before seasoning with black pepper and sea salt.
- Wash the chicken pieces and place in a greased ovenproof dish, just big enough to hold them. Pour over the sauce, ensuring the chicken is well covered.
- Cover with a double layer of tin foil and place in the fridge to marinate for at least 2 hours. Remove from the fridge so it is at room temperature when you are ready to cook.
- Meanwhile, wash your new potatoes. Whilst they are wet, place them in a bowl, drizzle with olive oil and season well. Add a generous sprinkle of paprika and combine until you have covered the potatoes in a paprika blush.
- Tip the potatoes onto your browning tray and place on the high rack. Set the temperature to 220°C and cook for 10–15 minutes. Then transfer to the low rack and turn down to 200°C. Place the chicken (with foil still intact) on the high rack. Cook for 30–40 minutes until the chicken and the potatoes are cooked to your requirements.
- Serve with green vegetables.

1–2 bulbs garlic, cloves peeled but left whole
300–400ml olive oil
Juice and zest of 2 lemons
2 tablespoons crème fraîche
1 teaspoon mustard
Black pepper
Sea salt
4–6 chicken breasts (depending on appetite!)
1kg new potatoes
Paprika

Gammon Steaks with Parsley Sauce and Mini Roasts

SERVES 4

1kg new potatoes, washed
Olive oil
Garlic and herb seasoning
Paprika
25g butter
25g plain flour or cornflour
500–600ml milk
Handful of parsley, freshly chopped
Black pepper
Sea salt
4 gammon steaks

- Place the potatoes on an oiled baking tray. Drizzle with olive oil and season with garlic and herb seasoning. Finish with a sprinkle of paprika. Shake the tray to ensure the potatoes are evenly covered. Add more olive oil if you think it is too dry.
- Set the halogen to 200°C. Place the potatoes on the high rack and cook for 30–40 minutes, until they are cooked and golden.
- Meanwhile, make the sauce by melting the butter in a saucepan on the hob over a medium heat. Add the flour and using a wooden spoon stir well to form a paste. Gradually add the milk and continue to stir. If lumps begin to form, swap the wooden spoon for a balloon whisk and whisk well. Continue to stir/whisk until the sauce starts to thicken. Add the parsley and season to taste. Remove from the heat.
- Set the halogen to 230°C. Move the potatoes to the low rack and place the gammon steaks on the grill rack as you are effectively going to grill them (see the section on grilling in Chapter 1 for tips).
- Brush the steaks lightly with olive oil. Cook for approximately 4–5 minutes on each side until they are cooked to your requirements. The cooking time depends on the size and thickness of the steaks.
- Whilst they are cooking, gently reheat the sauce on a low heat, ensuring it does not boil or it may catch and burn. If you are cooking vegetables to accompany the meal, you will need to have these ready.
- Remove the potatoes and steaks from the oven and onto your dinner plates. Pour the sauce over the steaks. Serve with peas or green vegetables.

Cheesy Tortillas with Guacamole and Beef Chilli

SERVES 4–6

Although I have included the Chilli here in the method, you really would be best preparing this recipe when you have some leftover Chilli, or why not double up a Chilli recipe and keep a stash in your freezer for when this recipe appeals. I have used readymade guacamole but you could make your own.

- In a large sauté pan on the hob, heat a little olive oil over a medium heat. Add the onion, garlic, chilli and pepper and cook until they start to soften.
- Add the mince and cook until brown. Add the spices and mushrooms, followed by the tomatoes and kidney beans. Cook for 10–15 minutes, adding stock or water if needed.
- When the Chilli is ready, you can begin to prepare the tortillas. Sandwich cheddar between 2 tortillas and repeat this for the remaining tortillas. Stack them onto a baking tray and place this on the high rack.
- Turn the halogen on to 200°C. Cook the tortillas for 10 minutes. After 3–4 minutes, you may want to move the top tortilla to the bottom of the pile to avoid it over cooking and to transfer the cooking to the others.
- Remove from the oven and cut into wedges.
- Serve on a plate with a spoonful of Chilli, a dollop of guacamole and sour cream.

Olive oil
1 onion, finely chopped
2–3 cloves garlic, crushed
½ chilli, finely chopped
½ red pepper
300g minced beef
1–2 teaspoons chilli powder
1 teaspoon paprika
4 mushrooms, chopped
1 tin chopped tomatoes
1 tin red kidney beans, washed and drained
6 tortillas
125g mature Cheddar, sliced
Guacamole
Sour cream

Seared Lamb with Sweet Potato Mash and Green Beans

SERVES 4

Olive oil
2 x 200g lamb neck
  fillets
4–6 sweet potatoes,
  peeled
200g green beans
Butter
Seasoning

- On your hob, heat a drizzle of olive oil in your sauté pan. Add the lamb and sear for 4–5 minutes over a high heat, turning until it is brown all over.
- Transfer to a baking tray. Place on the high rack and cook at 180°C for 10–12 minutes, depending on the thickness of the fillets and how you like your lamb cooked.
- Meanwhile, place the sweet potato in a saucepan of boiling water or steam until soft.
- Remove the lamb from the oven and wrap in foil to rest.
- Steam the green beans or boil until they are cooked to your taste – I normally cook them for 5–8 minutes.
- Mash the potato with a little butter. Season to taste.
- Place the lamb on a bed of potato mash and serve with the green beans.

Gammon Steaks with Leek and Cheese Crumble

- Place the leeks in a sauté pan, with half the butter and season with freshly ground black pepper. Place on the hob and cook at a medium heat until they start to soften.
- Meanwhile, prepare the sauce by melting the remaining butter. Stir in the flour and continue to stir whilst gradually adding milk. If you start to get lumps, use a balloon whisk.
- Once the sauce starts to thicken, add the grated cheese and wholegrain mustard. Remove from the heat when the cheese has melted.
- Place the leeks in an ovenproof dish. Pour on the sauce.
- Combine the breadcrumbs, hazelnuts, oats and Parmesan. Season to taste.
- Sprinkle the crumble mixture over the leeks.
- Place on the low rack and cook at 190°C for 10 minutes.
- You can cook your steaks on the hob, or you can grill them in the halogen using the grilling rack. Move the leek crumble to the base of the halogen. Place the grill rack over the top – you may need to use baking trays or similar to help you achieve this.
- Set the temperature to 250° and grill until the steaks are cooked, turning halfway through.
- Serve immediately with the crumble.

350g leeks, sliced
40g butter
Black pepper
20g plain flour or cornflour
450ml milk
120g mature cheese, grated
1 tablespoon whoegrain mustard
3 tablespoons home-prepared wholemeal breadcrumbs
30g hazlenuts, chopped
2 tablespoons oats
20g Parmesan cheese
Black pepper to taste
4 gammon steaks

Desserts

Dessert really is my favourite part of a meal and, yes, my waistline will vouch for me! This chapter contains traditional family favourites as well as some new ideas to tempt you. If you want to watch your calories, substitute cream for low-fat crème fraîche, thick Greek yoghurt (0% Total is the best), or fat-free plain yoghurt. Some people use quark, which is low in fat. I find it is best when mixed with a little yoghurt and a drop or two of vanilla extract.

Elderflower and Berry Healthy Brûlée

SERVES 4-6

100–150g selection of fresh berries (e.g. raspberries, strawberries, red currants, blueberries, blackcurrants)

1–2 tablespoons elderflower cordial

350–400g Greek yoghurt (I use Total 0%)

3 tablespoons low fat crème fraîche

1 teaspoon vanilla paste

1–2 teaspoons icing sugar (only if you have a sweet tooth)

3–4 tablespoons brown sugar

This is seriously yummy!

- Wash the berries. You may want to slice the strawberries in half if they are quite large. Place in an ovenproof dish. Drizzle with the elderflower cordial. Toss, ensuring they are evenly coated, and leave to one side.
- Mix the yoghurt and crème fraîche together in a bowl. Once combined, add the vanilla paste and icing sugar (if you have a sweet tooth) and stir well.
- Spoon the yoghurt mixture over the berries. Finish with a sprinkle of brown sugar – enough to form a generous layer to make the crème brûlée effect.
- Place in the halogen oven on the grill rack (see the section on grilling in Chapter 1 for tips). Turn to the highest setting (usually 250°C) and cook for 3–4 minutes, allowing the brown sugar to start melting and caramelising. The beauty of the halogen is that it allows you to see this cooking, therefore avoiding burning.
- Serve and enjoy!

Choca-Mocha Saucy Pudding

SERVES 4–6

You could make this in small ramekin dishes, but adjust the cooking time if you do.

- In your mixer, beat the sugar and butter together until creamy and fluffy. Gradually add the beaten eggs, milk and vanilla and mix well. Then add the flour and cocoa.
- Pour into a greased ovenproof dish (or ramekin dishes) and smooth over until flat.
- In a bowl or jug, mix the boiling water, sugar and coffee together and stir thoroughly until dissolved and lump free. Pour this over the sponge mixture.
- Place on the low rack and cook for 35–40 minutes at 175°C, until the sponge is firm to touch. (If you are using ramekins, cook for 20–25 minutes.)
- Serve with a dollop of Greek yoghurt or crème fraîche and enjoy!

115g sugar
115g butter
2 eggs, beaten
2 tablespoons milk
1 tablespoon vanilla essence or paste
100g self-raising flour
2 tablespoons cocoa
300ml boiling water
2 tablespoons sugar
1 tablespoon instant coffee
Greek yoghurt or crème fraîche to serve

Chocolate and Hazelnut Bread and Butter Pudding

SERVES 4–6

30g butter
4–6 slices of panettone
(if you don't have
this use stale white
bread)
40g hazelnuts,
chopped
100g chocolate chips
(I prefer to use
plain)
50g sugar
2 eggs, beaten
300ml milk
75ml cream (optional
– if you prefer not to
use cream, increase
the quantity of milk
to 375ml, whole milk
is creamier)
Crème fraîche or
clotted cream to
serve

An indulgent twist to a traditional favourite.

• Grease your ovenproof dish with butter. Butter your panettone slices and line the dish, sprinkling chopped hazelnuts, chocolate chips and sugar between the slices.

• In a jug, mix the eggs, milk and cream (if you are using it) together. Pour this over the bread mixture, pushing the bread down into the liquid where necessary. Then let this sit for about 10 minutes to absorb the milk.

• Push the bread down into the liquid and place the dish on the low rack. Cook for 30 minutes at 210°C until the top is golden and the base is almost set.

• Serve with a dollop of crème fraîche or for luxury and indulgence, some clotted cream!

Baked Banana Apples with Ricotta Cream

SERVES 4

I discovered this recipe in a 1970s good housekeeping book and thought it looked quite fun. I have adapted it to suit our tastes and it is perfect for the halogen. Serve with this delicious ricotta cream for some extra indulgence.

- Place the cored apples on a greased or lined baking tray.
- In a bowl, mix the banana, nutmeg, 1 teaspoon of cinnamon, lemon juice and sugar together. Fill the cores of the apples with the banana mixture.
- Place the apples on the high rack of your halogen and set the temperature to 190°C. Cook for 30–40 minutes until the apples are tender.
- While the apples are cooking, mix the ricotta and yoghurt with the vanilla, honey and ½ teaspoon of cinnamon.
- Remove the apples from the oven and place on your serving dish with a generous dollop of the ricotta cream.

4 cooking apples, cored
2–3 soft bananas, mashed
½ teaspoon nutmeg
1½ teaspoons cinnamon
15ml lemon juice
2 tablespoons brown sugar
110g ricotta
50ml Greek yoghurt
½ teaspoon vanilla extract
1 tablespoon clear runny honey

SERVES 4

600ml full-fat milk
4 eggs
50g sugar
1 teaspoon vanilla
  extract
Nutmeg, grated

Baked Egg Custard

This used to be my favourite when I was growing up and I still crave it when I'm in need of some comfort.

- In a saucepan or milk pan, heat the milk until it is very hot but not boiling.
- While that is coming to the heat (but don't leave it unattended otherwise the milk will boil over!), place the eggs, sugar and vanilla extract in a bowl and beat together. Slowly add the hot milk, stirring with a whisk until it is evenly distributed.
- Strain into an ovenproof bowl or dish or 4 ramekin dishes and sprinkle with nutmeg. Cover with foil if your halogen does not allow you to turn the fan to low.
- Place a large deep tray in the halogen, as you will be using this as a water bath. Place the ovenproof bowl containing the egg custard in the centre of this tray and fill the tray with hot water until it reaches halfway up the bowl or ramekin dishes.
- Set the temperature to 180°C and cook for 50–60 minutes until set. Ramekins may take slightly less time so keep an eye on them. It should be firm when set.
- Turn out when ready to serve or you can chill and serve cold.

Healthy Breakfast Kebabs

SERVES 2–3

- In a bowl, mix the honey and orange juice together. Sprinkle with a little cinnamon if you like the flavour.
- Soak the dried fruit in this mixture for at least 1 hour. Then drain the fruit and leave the juice to one side.
- When you are ready to cook, thread alternate fruits (fresh and dried) on your kebab skewers. (If you are using wooden skewers, make sure they are pre-soaked.)
- Place the skewers on the grill rack (see the section on grilling in Chapter 1 for tips). Set the temperature to 250°C and cook for 3–5 minutes each side.
- Serve with a drizzle of the honey and orange mixture and a dollop of natural yoghurt.

1–2 tablespoons runny honey
3–4 tablespoons orange juice
1 teaspoon cinnamon (optional)
Dried figs
Dried apricots
Dates
Prunes
Dried apple rings
Fresh banana
Fresh orange
Natural yoghurt to serve

500g cooking apples,
   peeled, cored and
   sliced
½ lemon, cut into
   wedges
2 tablespoons sugar
1 teaspoon cinnamon
   (optional)
75g honey-nut
   cornflakes (or
   ordinary cornflakes
   if you prefer)
30g butter
Crème fraîche or
   natural yoghurt to
   serve

Apple Nut Crunch

I love simple puddings that don't take too much messing
around but still give you a nice comforting dessert. This is
really popular with the kids and ideal for a warming dessert.

- Place the apple slices and lemon wedges in a pan on
  your hob and cook over a medium heat until the
  apples are soft. You may want to add a little water to
  prevent them from drying too much – about 4–5
  dessertspoons should be plenty. If you want to save
  washing up, cook them in an ovenproof/hob-proof
  shallow dish.
- Remove the lemon wedges and throw them away. Stir
  in the sugar and cinnamon and remove from the
  heat.
- If you are not already using a shallow ovenproof dish,
  transfer the apples into one now.
- Cover the cooked apple with the honey-nut
  cornflakes. Place the butter dotted randomly in
  amongst the cornflakes.
- Place on the grill rack (see the section on grilling in
  Chapter 1 for tips). Turn the heat to 240°C (you are
  effectively grilling the top) and cook for 5–8 minutes
  until golden.
- Serve immediately with a dollop of crème fraîche or
  natural yoghurt.

Simple Hot Chocolate Soufflés

This is so easy and takes very little time to make. Serve with a dollop of crème fraîche for a delicious indulgent pudding.

Butter, softened
4 teaspoons caster sugar
100g dark chocolate (at least 70% cocoa is best)
4 eggs, separated
50g caster sugar, plus 2 teaspoons extra
Cocoa powder or icing sugar to sprinkle
Crème fraîche to serve

- Rub a knob of butter around the inside of 4 ramekins to help prevent sticking. Sprinkle the caster sugar over the butter to form a layer. Shake off any residue sugar.
- Melt the chocolate using a bain marie or a bowl over a pan of hot water, making sure the hot water does not touch the base of the bowl. Alternatively you could melt it in a microwave.
- While the chocolate is melting, mix the egg yolks with 50g of caster sugar until they become light and fluffy. Add the melted chocolate and combine well.
- Whisk the egg whites until they form soft peaks. Add 2 teaspoons of caster sugar and whisk until it is thick.
- Add a spoonful of the egg whites to the chocolate. Once combined, fold in the remaining egg white.
- Spoon the mixture into the ramekin dishes and level the tops off.
- Place on the high rack and cook for 10 minutes at 180°C, or until firm to touch but slightly wobbly in the centre as you want them a bit gooey.
- Remove from the oven and sprinkle with cocoa or icing sugar. Serve immediately in the ramekin dishes with a side dollop of crème fraîche.

Baked Honey and Ginger Pears

SERVES 4

2–4 pears, peeled,
   halved and cored
Runny honey
1 teaspoon mixed
   spice
4–8 ginger biscuits
Vanilla ice-cream to
   serve

- Place the pears in a pan of water. Boil for 8–10 minutes.
- Place the pears on a browning tray (which comes with the halogen accessory pack) or non-stick tray. Drizzle with a small amount of honey – try to keep this within the centre of the pears, as if it escapes onto the tray it may burn.
- Set your halogen to 220°C and bake for 10–15 minutes.
- While this is cooking, crush your ginger biscuits. Place them in a freezer bag and gently bash with a rolling pin.
- Remove the pears from the oven and drizzle with more honey and a sprinkle of mixed spice. Cover with the crumbled ginger biscuits.
- Place back in the oven and cook for another 5–10 minutes or until soft.
- Serve with a generous dollop of vanilla ice-cream.

Puffed-up Apple Pie

SERVES 4

This recipe only uses a top for the pie as I find sometimes the pastry can be a bit doughy. However, if you want to add a bottom, simply add a lining of pastry and bake blind (i.e. bake the pastry covered with a layer of greaseproof and baking beans) for 10–15 minutes before adding the apple and the top. For added security you could brush the pastry bottom, once cooked, with egg white or sprinkle with semolina.

- Peel, chop and core the cooking apples. Place in a saucepan with 3–4 dessertspoons of water. Sprinkle with the sugar, cinnamon and sultanas. Cook slowly on your hob over a medium heat so the apples just start to soften – you don't want them too soggy.
- Once ready, place the apples in a deep ovenproof dish. Roll out your pastry to the required thickness – I would opt for approximately 3–5mm.
- Brush the edge of your dish with egg or milk. Carefully cut a strip off the edge of your rolled pastry, wide enough to cover the edge/lip of your dish. Carefully place this over the edge of the dish. Push down to secure and brush again with egg or milk.
- Use your rolling pin to lift the pastry and place it on the ovenproof dish. Push down at the edges to secure. Crimp the edges of the pastry, making sure it is secure. Cut off excess pastry.
- Using a sharp knife, make two small slits in the top of the pastry to allow the air to escape. Brush with egg or milk and sprinkle with a little sugar.
- Place on the high rack and set the temperature to 210°C. Cook for 20–25 minutes until the pastry is golden.
- Serve with custard or a dollop of cream or ice-cream.

4–5 cooking apples (Bramleys preferably)
2–3 dessertspoons sugar, depending on taste
2 teaspoons ground cinnamon (optional)
2 handfuls of sultanas (optional)
½ pack readymade puff or sweet shortcrust pastry
1 egg, beaten, or a little milk
Custard, cream or ice-cream to serve

300g golden syrup
25g butter
50ml double cream
   (optional)
2 eggs, beaten
100–150g
   breadcrumbs
1 x 18–20cm pastry
   case, pre-baked
Cream, crème fraîche
   or natural yoghurt to
   serve

Cheat's Treacle Tart

If you love treacle tart, why not try this simple recipe. Using a pre-baked pastry case saves time and avoids soggy bottom pastry! This recipe is perfect for the 18–20cm pastry cases found in supermarkets.

- In a saucepan on your hob, gently heat the golden syrup over a medium heat until it becomes runny. Add the butter and stir well. Add the cream (if you are using it) and the beaten egg and combine well.
- Add the breadcrumbs and stir well. You want a fluid consistency, not thick and lumpy, but with enough texture to give the golden syrup body. Pour into the pastry case.
- Place on the high rack and cook at 170°C for 30 minutes. If your tart needs to be cooked for longer, turn the temperature down to 150°C and cook at 5-minute intervals, checking as you go to avoid burning. The pie should be firm and golden.
- Serve with a dollop of cream, crème fraîche or natural yoghurt.

Rich Semolina Pudding

I adore these old-fashioned puddings. This is simple to make and gives a comforting hug on a winter's evening.

- Place the milk in a saucepan and heat on your hob over a medium heat until very hot. Then add the semolina and sugar and bring to the boil, stirring constantly. The semolina will start to thicken – don't allow it to stick or burn.
- Remove from the heat and add all the remaining ingredients (reserving a little orange zest).
- Pour into your ovenproof dish. Sprinkle with a little extra orange zest and some nutmeg and brown sugar. Place on the high rack and cook at 180°C for 10–15 minutes.
- Serve immediately.

SERVES 4

600ml milk
60g semolina
60g caster sugar
Zest of 1 orange
   (finely grated)
2 egg yolks
60g sultanas
Nutmeg
Brown sugar

200g apricots
2 tablespoons water
(or cognac if you are
feeling
adventurous!)
1 tablespoon brown
sugar
110g butter
110g caster sugar
2 eggs, beaten
1 teaspoon vanilla
extract
110g self-raising flour
Apricot jam
Double cream to serve

Hot Vanilla and Apricot Sponge

- Place the apricots into an ovenproof dish. Drizzle with the water or cognac and sprinkle with the brown sugar.
- Place the dish on the high rack, set the temperature to 200°C and cook for 10 minutes.
- Meanwhile, in a mixing bowl, beat the butter and sugar until pale and fluffy. Add the beaten eggs and vanilla extract and beat again. Sift in the self-raising flour and fold the mixture carefully.
- Line a sponge tin (or use liners). I use an approximately 18cm-deep sponge tin.
- Pour in the cake mixture and flatten with a palette knife.
- Remove the apricots from the medium rack and place on the low rack. Place the cake on the high rack and set the temperature to 180°C.
- Bake the sponge for 20–25 minutes, or until it is cooked – it should spring back when touched and be coming away slightly from the edges of the tin.
- Remove the sponge from the oven. Turn out onto a plate and immediately spread with apricot jam.
- Carefully spoon on the apricots. Serve with dollops of double cream.

Cheat's Chocolate and Banana Pancakes

SERVES 2

So simple – perfect for a quick and easy dessert. You could make your own pancakes but, to be honest, readymade ones taste just as good and oh so easy. This recipe serves two, but you can double or treble up and cook in an ovenproof dish.

2 readymade pancakes (large ones, not the small American-style pancakes)
100g dark chocolate
70ml water
2 capfuls dark rum
1 tablespoon caster sugar
1–2 bananas
Cream, crème fraîche or ice-cream to serve

- Stack the pancakes on the high rack. (If you are cooking several, you may want to pop some baking parchment between the layers and rotate them whilst cooking to prevent the top one from overcooking.)
- Turn the halogen on to 190°C and cook for 8–10 minutes.
- Meanwhile, place the chocolate, water, rum and caster sugar in a saucepan and cook on your hob until you have a smooth sauce. Don't have the heat too high as it will burn.
- Place each hot pancake on the work surface. Place the banana on one edge, drizzle with the sauce and roll up into a sausage. Put in your ovenproof dish.
- Place the dish on the high rack, set the temperature to 190°C and cook for another 5 minutes.
- Serve immediately with cream, crème fraîche or ice-cream and a drizzle more of the lovely sauce.

Why not try some other fillings – here are some suggestions:
- **Apple and Mincemeat Pancakes** – spread the pancakes with stewed apple and dollops of mincemeat. Serve with clotted cream.
- **Healthy Peach and Raspberry Pancakes** – place the fruit in the pancake as above, add a few dollops of crème fraîche and cook as described above. Serve with a sprinkle of icing sugar and a dollop of low-fat crème fraîche.

Chocolate, Banana and Brazil Nut Tiramisu

SERVES 4–6

150–200ml strong coffee

150g Greek yoghurt

150g double cream

50g cream cheese

1 teaspoon vanilla extract

50g brazil nuts, crushed

6–8 sponge fingers

75g dark chocolate

3–4 bananas, chopped

2–3 teaspoons cocoa

- Make the coffee and leave it to cool.
- In a bowl, mix the yoghurt, cream, cream cheese and vanilla extract together.
- Place the crushed brazil nuts on a baking tray. Put this on the grill rack (see the section on grilling in Chapter 1 for tips). Grill *very carefully* at 240°C for 2–3 minutes until they start to darken. You will need to watch this as they can burn easily.
- You can make this in one large dish or individual dishes. This recipe, for ease, uses one dish. Place the sponge fingers in the bottom of the dish. Pour over the coffee and allow to soak for at least 5 minutes. You could start to melt your chocolate (use a bowl over a saucepan of boiling water, or the microwave), whilst you are waiting.
- Pour half the yoghurt mixture over the sponges. Then place the chopped banana. Pour half the melted chocolate into the remaining yoghurt mixture and fold lightly (you want a ripple effect). Spoon this over the banana.
- Finish with a sprinkle of cocoa and the chopped nuts and drizzle with the remaining dark chocolate.
- Place in the fridge for at least 1 hour or until you are ready to eat.

Apple, Sultana and Cinnamon Mini Cakes

MAKES 4–6
(depending on size of cases)

- Cream the butter and sugar together until pale and fluffy.
- Add the egg a little at a time and continue to beat well.
- Sift the flour and cinnamon and fold into the mixture gently. Add the sultanas and combine well.
- When thoroughly mixed, place half the mixture into silicon cupcake cases. I have not been able to find a round muffin tray so I use silicon muffin cases and place these on the halogen baking trays that come with the accessory packs. Press the cake mixture down to ensure the bottom of the silicon cases are covered.
- Using a teaspoon, place a spoonful of stewed apple in the centre of each case. Finish with the remaining cake mixture.
- Place on the low rack and cook for 12–18 minutes at 190°C. The cakes should be firm and spring back when touched.
- Serve warm with some custard.

55g butter
55g sugar
1 egg, beaten
55g self-raising flour
1 teaspoon cinnamon
20g sultanas
50g stewed apple
Custard to serve

Berry Ripple Mousse with Melting Biscuits

225g butter
50g icing sugar
½ teaspoon vanilla extract
175g self-raising flour
50g cornflour
250g strawberries
100g raspberries
2 tablespoons caster sugar
75g cream cheese
150g double cream
100g Greek yoghurt
1 teaspoon vanilla extract

- Beat the butter and icing sugar together. Add ½ teaspoon of vanilla extract and combine.
- Sift the flour and cornflour and fold in.
- Place baking parchment on a baking tray. Using a teaspoon, place dollops of the mixture evenly over the tray.
- Bake on the low rack for 10–12 minutes at 180°C until golden and just firm but not hard.
- Remove the biscuits from the oven and leave on the tray for a couple of minutes before placing on a cooling rack.
- Place two-thirds of the strawberries and raspberries in an ovenproof dish. Sprinkle with the sugar and place on the high rack.
- Cook at 180°C for 5 minutes. Remove and leave to one side to cool.
- Meanwhile, mix the cream cheese, cream, yoghurt and vanilla extract together. Fold in half of the cooked berries.
- Prepare individual serving glasses by placing some of the fresh fruit in the bottom of the glasses. Top with a little of the yoghurt mixture, followed by the cooked berries, repeating until you almost fill the glass. Finish with the fresh berries.
- Serve with 3 or 4 biscuits per serving.

Cuban-style Baked Bananas

SERVES 4

- Peel the bananas and cut them in half lengthways. Cut each length in half widthways.
- Place the bananas in a greased ovenproof dish. Top with the raisins and pecan nuts. Don't worry if you have to layer this, it will be fine.
- Dollop small amounts of butter across the top of the nuts, before drizzling with honey and finishing with the ground cinnamon.
- Place on the low rack and cook at 200°C for 20 minutes. Lift the lid of the halogen and carefully add the rum. Cook again for another 5 minutes.
- Serve with a dollop of cream.

3 bananas
50g raisins
75g pecan nuts
50g butter
3 tablespoons runny honey
2 teaspoons ground cinnamon
2–3 tablespoons rum
Cream to serve

Simple Chocolate and Banana Tortilla

SERVES 2–4

2 tortillas
Chocolate spread
1–2 bananas, sliced
Handful of chocolate
  chips (optional)
Cream, ice-cream or
  crème fraîche to
  serve

Kids crying out for a quick dessert? – this is really easy and takes minutes to prepare.

- Spread one of the tortillas with chocolate spread. Cover this with the banana slices and sprinkle with the chocolate chips. Place the remaining tortilla on top and press down firmly.
- Place on the high rack at 210°C for 8–10 minutes.
- Remove carefully as it is very hot. Place on a serving dish and cut into 6 slices.
- Serve on its own or with a dollop of cream, ice–cream or crème fraîche.

Raspberry Cream Slice

SERVES 4–6

So simple, yet deliciously decadent.

Roll of puff pastry
Raspberry jam
200ml double cream,
   whipped
200g fresh raspberries
Icing sugar

- Unroll your puff pastry. Using a rolling pin, roll again so it is thinner.
- Use a ruler and cut as many equally-sized rectangles as you can – roughly 5cm by 10cm should be perfect. Aim for 12, 15 or 18 as you will be using 3 per slice.
- Place these on a greased or lined baking tray (you will probably have to cook in two batches). Prick with a fork.
- Place on the high rack and cook at 210°C for 10–15 minutes until the pastry is golden and perfectly cooked. If you are unsure about the base of the pastry, you can carefully turn them over and cook for another few minutes. You want light, crisp pastry rectangles – not soggy.
- When the pastry is cooked, place on a cooling rack and leave until perfectly cool.
- When you are ready to assemble, place the pastry in sets of three. Spread raspberry jam on the top of two of the pastry pieces from each group (leaving one from each set to one side).
- Follow this with a piping of whipped cream. (If you don't want to pipe it, carefully spoon on and spread well, without spilling over the edges.)
- Top the cream with raspberries.
- Now you are ready to stack. Place one of the fruit and cream slices on a plate to use as the base. Follow this with the remaining cream and raspberry slice. Finish with the plain pastry top. Sprinkle with icing sugar. Repeat for all the other slices.
- Serve and enjoy!

Cherry Pie

SERVES 4

600g stoned cherries
3–4 tablespoons sugar,
  depending on taste
1 teaspoon cornflour
½ pack readymade puff
  or sweet shortcrust
  pastry
1 egg, beaten or a
  little milk to brush
Custard, cream or ice-
  cream to serve

- Place the cherries in a deep ovenproof pie dish. Sprinkle with sugar and cornflour and combine well.
- Place on the high rack and cook at 200°C for 10 minutes.
- Meanwhile, roll out your pastry to the required thickness – I would opt for approximately 3–5mm.
- Remove the dish from the oven. Brush the edge of the dish with egg or milk. Carefully cut a strip off the edge of your rolled pastry, wide enough to cover the edge/lip of the dish. Carefully place this over the edge of the dish. Press down to secure. Brush again with egg or milk.
- With your rolling pin, lift up the pastry as this makes it easier to handle. Unroll onto the dish. Push down at the edges to secure. Then go around the edges of the pastry with a crimping motion, making sure it is secure. Cut off excess pastry – you could use this to decorate the top of the pie with leaf shapes or similar.
- Using a sharp knife, make two small slits in the top of the pastry to allow the air to escape. Brush with egg or milk and sprinkle with a little sugar.
- Place on the high rack and set the temperature to 210°C. Cook for 20–25 minutes until the pastry is golden.
- Serve with custard or a dollop of cream or ice-cream.

Bakewell Tart

This tart uses a pre-baked pastry case as the halogen can often undercook pastry bases. You can buy these from the shop or make it yourself. This recipe uses a 20–22cm pastry case.

- Place a layer of raspberry jam in your pastry case. Leave to one side.
- In a bowl, beat the butter and sugar together until light and fluffy.
- Beat in the egg, followed by the flour, ground almonds and almond essence.
- Spoon this mixture over the jam and spread until even.
- Set the halogen to 180°C. Place on the high rack and cook for 20–25 minutes, or until the sponge is golden and cooked thoroughly.
- Remove from the oven and cool.
- Mix up the icing sugar, adding a few drops of water at a time until you have a perfect consistency.
- Melt the chocolate (if using) in the microwave or a bowl over a saucepan of hot water.
- When the tart is cool, spread with a layer of icing.
- Using a piping bag with a thin nozzle, pipe lines of chocolate, approximately 2cm apart horizontally across the top of the tart. Using a sharp knife, pull down vertically across the piped chocolate in a straight line – this will pull the chocolate down to form a lovely criss-cross pattern. Repeat, approximately 2cm apart, across the cake.
- Serve with a lovely cup of tea.

SERVES 6–8

1 x 20–22cm pastry case, pre-baked
Raspberry jam
55g butter
55g sugar
1 egg, beaten
30g self-raising flour
50g ground almonds
Almond essence
100g icing sugar
15–20ml cold water
25g melted chocolate (optional)

Pineapple and Cinnamon Tarts

SERVES 4–6

½ roll puff pastry
2–3 tablespoons brown sugar
300g pineapple rings
1–2 teaspoons ground cinnamon
Cream to serve

- Cut the rolled puff pastry into circles of approximately 8–10cm. Place on a greased baking tray. Prick with a fork and sprinkle with brown sugar.
- Place on the high rack and cook at 200°C for 10 minutes.
- Meanwhile, carefully cut half of the pineapple rings in half, to make two thinner rings per original ring.
- Remove the pastry from the oven. Place the thinner rings randomly onto the pastry, leaving the thicker rings for later.
- Sprinkle with a generous amount of brown sugar. Sprinkle with cinnamon.
- Put back in the oven and cook for another 15 minutes until the pastry is cooked and the pineapple golden.
- Serve with the extra pineapple and dollops of cream.

Fruity Gooey Kebabs

You can use whatever fruit you fancy, but remember it will be hot so soft fruit may not work.

- Soak your skewers if you are using wooden ones.
- Then take your skewers and randomly thread fruit and marshmallows onto them.
- Place on the grilling rack (see the section on grilling in Chapter 1 for tips). Set the halogen to 250°C and grill for 3–4 minutes each side.
- Remove and serve. Why not melt some chocolate and drizzle over the grilled kebabs!

SERVES 4–6

Marshmallows
1–2 bananas
1–2 peaches
1–2 nectarines
1 apple
Chocolate to serve (optional)

Blackberry, Apple and Almond Bake

SERVES 4–6

75g blackberries
4–5 Bramley cooking
   apples, peeled and
   diced
2–3 tablespoons sugar
   (or to taste)
55g butter
55g sugar
1 egg, beaten
30g self-raising flour
50g ground almonds
Almond essence
Cream, crème fraîche
   or ice-cream to serve

- Place the blackberries and apple in a saucepan on your hob. Add 4 tablespoons of water and 2–3 tablespoons of sugar.
- Heat slowly until the apple starts to soften, but still remains in chunks. Then remove from the heat and place in a deep ovenproof dish.
- In a bowl, beat the butter and sugar together until light and fluffy.
- Beat in the egg, followed by the flour, ground almonds and almond essence.
- Spoon this mixture over the apple and spread until even. If you find this difficult, simply dollop little spoonfuls of the cake mixture around the top as close together as you can – it will blend in during cooking.
- Set the halogen to 180°C. Place on the high rack and cook for 20–25 minutes, or until the sponge is golden and cooked thoroughly.
- Remove from the oven and serve with a dollop of cream, crème fraîche or ice-cream.

Index